CS-41   GENERAL APTITUDE AND ABILITIES SERIES

This is your
PASSBOOK for...

Report Writing

Test Preparation Study Guide
Questions & Answers

COPYRIGHT NOTICE

This book is SOLELY intended for, is sold ONLY to, and its use is RESTRICTED to individual, bona fide applicants or candidates who qualify by virtue of having seriously filed applications for appropriate license, certificate, professional and/or promotional advancement, higher school matriculation, scholarship, or other legitimate requirements of education and/or governmental authorities.

This book is NOT intended for use, class instruction, tutoring, training, duplication, copying, reprinting, excerption, or adaptation, etc., by:

1) Other publishers
2) Proprietors and/or Instructors of "Coaching" and/or Preparatory Courses
3) Personnel and/or Training Divisions of commercial, industrial, and governmental organizations
4) Schools, colleges, or universities and/or their departments and staffs, including teachers and other personnel
5) Testing Agencies or Bureaus
6) Study groups which seek by the purchase of a single volume to copy and/or duplicate and/or adapt this material for use by the group as a whole without having purchased individual volumes for each of the members of the group
7) Et al.

Such persons would be in violation of appropriate Federal and State statutes.

PROVISION OF LICENSING AGREEMENTS – Recognized educational, commercial, industrial, and governmental institutions and organizations, and others legitimately engaged in educational pursuits, including training, testing, and measurement activities, may address request for a licensing agreement to the copyright owners, who will determine whether, and under what conditions, including fees and charges, the materials in this book may be used them. In other words, a licensing facility exists for the legitimate use of the material in this book on other than an individual basis. However, it is asseverated and affirmed here that the material in this book CANNOT be used without the receipt of the express permission of such a licensing agreement from the Publishers. Inquiries re licensing should be addressed to the company, attention rights and permissions department.

All rights reserved, including the right of reproduction in whole or in part, in any form or by any means, electronic or mechanical, including photocopying, recording, or by any information storage and retrieval system, without permission in writing from the Publisher.

Copyright © 2024 by
National Learning Corporation

212 Michael Drive, Syosset, NY 11791
(516) 921-8888 • www.passbooks.com
E-mail: info@passbooks.com

PUBLISHED IN THE UNITED STATES OF AMERICA

PASSBOOK® SERIES

THE *PASSBOOK® SERIES* has been created to prepare applicants and candidates for the ultimate academic battlefield – the examination room.

At some time in our lives, each and every one of us may be required to take an examination – for validation, matriculation, admission, qualification, registration, certification, or licensure.

Based on the assumption that every applicant or candidate has met the basic formal educational standards, has taken the required number of courses, and read the necessary texts, the *PASSBOOK® SERIES* furnishes the one special preparation which may assure passing with confidence, instead of failing with insecurity. Examination questions – together with answers – are furnished as the basic vehicle for study so that the mysteries of the examination and its compounding difficulties may be eliminated or diminished by a sure method.

This book is meant to help you pass your examination provided that you qualify and are serious in your objective.

The entire field is reviewed through the huge store of content information which is succinctly presented through a provocative and challenging approach – the question-and-answer method.

A climate of success is established by furnishing the correct answers at the end of each test.

You soon learn to recognize types of questions, forms of questions, and patterns of questioning. You may even begin to anticipate expected outcomes.

You perceive that many questions are repeated or adapted so that you can gain acute insights, which may enable you to score many sure points.

You learn how to confront new questions, or types of questions, and to attack them confidently and work out the correct answers.

You note objectives and emphases, and recognize pitfalls and dangers, so that you may make positive educational adjustments.

Moreover, you are kept fully informed in relation to new concepts, methods, practices, and directions in the field.

You discover that you are actually taking the examination all the time: you are preparing for the examination by "taking" an examination, not by reading extraneous and/or supererogatory textbooks.

In short, this PASSBOOK®, used directedly, should be an important factor in helping you to pass your test.

REPORT WRITING

The General Aptitude and Abilities Series provides functional, intensive test practice and drill in the basic skills and areas common to many civil service, general aptitude and achievement examinations necessary for entrance into schools or occupations.

Passbooks in this series use a variety of question types, and other applicable items like charts, graphs, illustrations and more, to prepare candidates for testing in particular subject areas. This Passbook features a wide range of questions covering report writing; written communication; and more.

HOW TO TAKE A TEST

I. YOU MUST PASS AN EXAMINATION

A. *WHAT EVERY CANDIDATE SHOULD KNOW*

Examination applicants often ask us for help in preparing for the written test. What can I study in advance? What kinds of questions will be asked? How will the test be given? How will the papers be graded?

As an applicant for a civil service examination, you may be wondering about some of these things. Our purpose here is to suggest effective methods of advance study and to describe civil service examinations.

Your chances for success on this examination can be increased if you know how to prepare. Those "pre-examination jitters" can be reduced if you know what to expect. You can even experience an adventure in good citizenship if you know why civil service exams are given.

B. *WHY ARE CIVIL SERVICE EXAMINATIONS GIVEN?*

Civil service examinations are important to you in two ways. As a citizen, you want public jobs filled by employees who know how to do their work. As a job seeker, you want a fair chance to compete for that job on an equal footing with other candidates. The best-known means of accomplishing this two-fold goal is the competitive examination.

Exams are widely publicized throughout the nation. They may be administered for jobs in federal, state, city, municipal, town or village governments or agencies.

Any citizen may apply, with some limitations, such as the age or residence of applicants. Your experience and education may be reviewed to see whether you meet the requirements for the particular examination. When these requirements exist, they are reasonable and applied consistently to all applicants. Thus, a competitive examination may cause you some uneasiness now, but it is your privilege and safeguard.

C. *HOW ARE CIVIL SERVICE EXAMS DEVELOPED?*

Examinations are carefully written by trained technicians who are specialists in the field known as "psychological measurement," in consultation with recognized authorities in the field of work that the test will cover. These experts recommend the subject matter areas or skills to be tested; only those knowledges or skills important to your success on the job are included. The most reliable books and source materials available are used as references. Together, the experts and technicians judge the difficulty level of the questions.

Test technicians know how to phrase questions so that the problem is clearly stated. Their ethics do not permit "trick" or "catch" questions. Questions may have been tried out on sample groups, or subjected to statistical analysis, to determine their usefulness.

Written tests are often used in combination with performance tests, ratings of training and experience, and oral interviews. All of these measures combine to form the best-known means of finding the right person for the right job.

II. HOW TO PASS THE WRITTEN TEST

A. NATURE OF THE EXAMINATION

To prepare intelligently for civil service examinations, you should know how they differ from school examinations you have taken. In school you were assigned certain definite pages to read or subjects to cover. The examination questions were quite detailed and usually emphasized memory. Civil service exams, on the other hand, try to discover your present ability to perform the duties of a position, plus your potentiality to learn these duties. In other words, a civil service exam attempts to predict how successful you will be. Questions cover such a broad area that they cannot be as minute and detailed as school exam questions.

In the public service similar kinds of work, or positions, are grouped together in one "class." This process is known as *position-classification*. All the positions in a class are paid according to the salary range for that class. One class title covers all of these positions, and they are all tested by the same examination.

B. FOUR BASIC STEPS

1) Study the announcement

How, then, can you know what subjects to study? Our best answer is: "Learn as much as possible about the class of positions for which you've applied." The exam will test the knowledge, skills and abilities needed to do the work.

Your most valuable source of information about the position you want is the official exam announcement. This announcement lists the training and experience qualifications. Check these standards and apply only if you come reasonably close to meeting them.

The brief description of the position in the examination announcement offers some clues to the subjects which will be tested. Think about the job itself. Review the duties in your mind. Can you perform them, or are there some in which you are rusty? Fill in the blank spots in your preparation.

Many jurisdictions preview the written test in the exam announcement by including a section called "Knowledge and Abilities Required," "Scope of the Examination," or some similar heading. Here you will find out specifically what fields will be tested.

2) Review your own background

Once you learn in general what the position is all about, and what you need to know to do the work, ask yourself which subjects you already know fairly well and which need improvement. You may wonder whether to concentrate on improving your strong areas or on building some background in your fields of weakness. When the announcement has specified "some knowledge" or "considerable knowledge," or has used adjectives like "beginning principles of…" or "advanced … methods," you can get a clue as to the number and difficulty of questions to be asked in any given field. More questions, and hence broader coverage, would be included for those subjects which are more important in the work. Now weigh your strengths and weaknesses against the job requirements and prepare accordingly.

3) Determine the level of the position

Another way to tell how intensively you should prepare is to understand the level of the job for which you are applying. Is it the entering level? In other words, is this the position in which beginners in a field of work are hired? Or is it an intermediate or advanced level? Sometimes this is indicated by such words as "Junior" or "Senior" in the class title. Other jurisdictions use Roman numerals to designate the level – Clerk I, Clerk II, for example. The word "Supervisor" sometimes appears in the title. If the level is not indicated by the title, check the description of duties. Will you be working under very close supervision, or will you have responsibility for independent decisions in this work?

4) Choose appropriate study materials

Now that you know the subjects to be examined and the relative amount of each subject to be covered, you can choose suitable study materials. For beginning level jobs, or even advanced ones, if you have a pronounced weakness in some aspect of your training, read a modern, standard textbook in that field. Be sure it is up to date and has general coverage. Such books are normally available at your library, and the librarian will be glad to help you locate one. For entry-level positions, questions of appropriate difficulty are chosen – neither highly advanced questions, nor those too simple. Such questions require careful thought but not advanced training.

If the position for which you are applying is technical or advanced, you will read more advanced, specialized material. If you are already familiar with the basic principles of your field, elementary textbooks would waste your time. Concentrate on advanced textbooks and technical periodicals. Think through the concepts and review difficult problems in your field.

These are all general sources. You can get more ideas on your own initiative, following these leads. For example, training manuals and publications of the government agency which employs workers in your field can be useful, particularly for technical and professional positions. A letter or visit to the government department involved may result in more specific study suggestions, and certainly will provide you with a more definite idea of the exact nature of the position you are seeking.

III. KINDS OF TESTS

Tests are used for purposes other than measuring knowledge and ability to perform specified duties. For some positions, it is equally important to test ability to make adjustments to new situations or to profit from training. In others, basic mental abilities not dependent on information are essential. Questions which test these things may not appear as pertinent to the duties of the position as those which test for knowledge and information. Yet they are often highly important parts of a fair examination. For very general questions, it is almost impossible to help you direct your study efforts. What we can do is to point out some of the more common of these general abilities needed in public service positions and describe some typical questions.

1) General information

Broad, general information has been found useful for predicting job success in some kinds of work. This is tested in a variety of ways, from vocabulary lists to questions about current events. Basic background in some field of work, such as sociology or economics, may be sampled in a group of questions. Often these are principles which have become familiar to most persons through exposure rather than through formal training. It is difficult to advise you how to study for these questions; being alert to the world around you is our best suggestion.

2) Verbal ability

An example of an ability needed in many positions is verbal or language ability. Verbal ability is, in brief, the ability to use and understand words. Vocabulary and grammar tests are typical measures of this ability. Reading comprehension or paragraph interpretation questions are common in many kinds of civil service tests. You are given a paragraph of written material and asked to find its central meaning.

3) Numerical ability

Number skills can be tested by the familiar arithmetic problem, by checking paired lists of numbers to see which are alike and which are different, or by interpreting charts and graphs. In the latter test, a graph may be printed in the test booklet which you are asked to use as the basis for answering questions.

4) Observation

A popular test for law-enforcement positions is the observation test. A picture is shown to you for several minutes, then taken away. Questions about the picture test your ability to observe both details and larger elements.

5) Following directions

In many positions in the public service, the employee must be able to carry out written instructions dependably and accurately. You may be given a chart with several columns, each column listing a variety of information. The questions require you to carry out directions involving the information given in the chart.

6) Skills and aptitudes

Performance tests effectively measure some manual skills and aptitudes. When the skill is one in which you are trained, such as typing or shorthand, you can practice. These tests are often very much like those given in business school or high school courses. For many of the other skills and aptitudes, however, no short-time preparation can be made. Skills and abilities natural to you or that you have developed throughout your lifetime are being tested.

Many of the general questions just described provide all the data needed to answer the questions and ask you to use your reasoning ability to find the answers. Your best preparation for these tests, as well as for tests of facts and ideas, is to be at your physical and mental best. You, no doubt, have your own methods of getting into an exam-taking mood and keeping "in shape." The next section lists some ideas on this subject.

IV. KINDS OF QUESTIONS

Only rarely is the "essay" question, which you answer in narrative form, used in civil service tests. Civil service tests are usually of the short-answer type. Full instructions for answering these questions will be given to you at the examination. But in case this is your first experience with short-answer questions and separate answer sheets, here is what you need to know:

1) Multiple-choice Questions

Most popular of the short-answer questions is the "multiple choice" or "best answer" question. It can be used, for example, to test for factual knowledge, ability to solve problems or judgment in meeting situations found at work.

A multiple-choice question is normally one of three types—
- It can begin with an incomplete statement followed by several possible endings. You are to find the one ending which *best* completes the statement, although some of the others may not be entirely wrong.
- It can also be a complete statement in the form of a question which is answered by choosing one of the statements listed.

- It can be in the form of a problem – again you select the best answer.

Here is an example of a multiple-choice question with a discussion which should give you some clues as to the method for choosing the right answer:

When an employee has a complaint about his assignment, the action which will *best* help him overcome his difficulty is to
   A. discuss his difficulty with his coworkers
   B. take the problem to the head of the organization
   C. take the problem to the person who gave him the assignment
   D. say nothing to anyone about his complaint

In answering this question, you should study each of the choices to find which is best. Consider choice "A" – Certainly an employee may discuss his complaint with fellow employees, but no change or improvement can result, and the complaint remains unresolved. Choice "B" is a poor choice since the head of the organization probably does not know what assignment you have been given, and taking your problem to him is known as "going over the head" of the supervisor. The supervisor, or person who made the assignment, is the person who can clarify it or correct any injustice. Choice "C" is, therefore, correct. To say nothing, as in choice "D," is unwise. Supervisors have and interest in knowing the problems employees are facing, and the employee is seeking a solution to his problem.

2) True/False Questions

The "true/false" or "right/wrong" form of question is sometimes used. Here a complete statement is given. Your job is to decide whether the statement is right or wrong.

SAMPLE: A roaming cell-phone call to a nearby city costs less than a non-roaming call to a distant city.

This statement is wrong, or false, since roaming calls are more expensive.

This is not a complete list of all possible question forms, although most of the others are variations of these common types. You will always get complete directions for answering questions. Be sure you understand *how* to mark your answers – ask questions until you do.

V. RECORDING YOUR ANSWERS

Computer terminals are used more and more today for many different kinds of exams.
For an examination with very few applicants, you may be told to record your answers in the test booklet itself. Separate answer sheets are much more common. If this separate answer sheet is to be scored by machine – and this is often the case – it is highly important that you mark your answers correctly in order to get credit.
An electronic scoring machine is often used in civil service offices because of the speed with which papers can be scored. Machine-scored answer sheets must be marked with a pencil, which will be given to you. This pencil has a high graphite content which responds to the electronic scoring machine. As a matter of fact, stray dots may register as answers, so do not let your pencil rest on the answer sheet while you are pondering the correct answer. Also, if your pencil lead breaks or is otherwise defective, ask for another.

Since the answer sheet will be dropped in a slot in the scoring machine, be careful not to bend the corners or get the paper crumpled.

The answer sheet normally has five vertical columns of numbers, with 30 numbers to a column. These numbers correspond to the question numbers in your test booklet. After each number, going across the page are four or five pairs of dotted lines. These short dotted lines have small letters or numbers above them. The first two pairs may also have a "T" or "F" above the letters. This indicates that the first two pairs only are to be used if the questions are of the true-false type. If the questions are multiple choice, disregard the "T" and "F" and pay attention only to the small letters or numbers.

Answer your questions in the manner of the sample that follows:

32. The largest city in the United States is
    A. Washington, D.C.
    B. New York City
    C. Chicago
    D. Detroit
    E. San Francisco

1) Choose the answer you think is best. (New York City is the largest, so "B" is correct.)
2) Find the row of dotted lines numbered the same as the question you are answering. (Find row number 32)
3) Find the pair of dotted lines corresponding to the answer. (Find the pair of lines under the mark "B.")
4) Make a solid black mark between the dotted lines.

VI. BEFORE THE TEST

Common sense will help you find procedures to follow to get ready for an examination. Too many of us, however, overlook these sensible measures. Indeed, nervousness and fatigue have been found to be the most serious reasons why applicants fail to do their best on civil service tests. Here is a list of reminders:

- Begin your preparation early – Don't wait until the last minute to go scurrying around for books and materials or to find out what the position is all about.
- Prepare continuously – An hour a night for a week is better than an all-night cram session. This has been definitely established. What is more, a night a week for a month will return better dividends than crowding your study into a shorter period of time.
- Locate the place of the exam – You have been sent a notice telling you when and where to report for the examination. If the location is in a different town or otherwise unfamiliar to you, it would be well to inquire the best route and learn something about the building.
- Relax the night before the test – Allow your mind to rest. Do not study at all that night. Plan some mild recreation or diversion; then go to bed early and get a good night's sleep.
- Get up early enough to make a leisurely trip to the place for the test – This way unforeseen events, traffic snarls, unfamiliar buildings, etc. will not upset you.
- Dress comfortably – A written test is not a fashion show. You will be known by number and not by name, so wear something comfortable.

- Leave excess paraphernalia at home – Shopping bags and odd bundles will get in your way. You need bring only the items mentioned in the official notice you received; usually everything you need is provided. Do not bring reference books to the exam. They will only confuse those last minutes and be taken away from you when in the test room.
- Arrive somewhat ahead of time – If because of transportation schedules you must get there very early, bring a newspaper or magazine to take your mind off yourself while waiting.
- Locate the examination room – When you have found the proper room, you will be directed to the seat or part of the room where you will sit. Sometimes you are given a sheet of instructions to read while you are waiting. Do not fill out any forms until you are told to do so; just read them and be prepared.
- Relax and prepare to listen to the instructions
- If you have any physical problem that may keep you from doing your best, be sure to tell the test administrator. If you are sick or in poor health, you really cannot do your best on the exam. You can come back and take the test some other time.

VII. AT THE TEST

The day of the test is here and you have the test booklet in your hand. The temptation to get going is very strong. Caution! There is more to success than knowing the right answers. You must know how to identify your papers and understand variations in the type of short-answer question used in this particular examination. Follow these suggestions for maximum results from your efforts:

1) Cooperate with the monitor

The test administrator has a duty to create a situation in which you can be as much at ease as possible. He will give instructions, tell you when to begin, check to see that you are marking your answer sheet correctly, and so on. He is not there to guard you, although he will see that your competitors do not take unfair advantage. He wants to help you do your best.

2) Listen to all instructions

Don't jump the gun! Wait until you understand all directions. In most civil service tests you get more time than you need to answer the questions. So don't be in a hurry. Read each word of instructions until you clearly understand the meaning. Study the examples, listen to all announcements and follow directions. Ask questions if you do not understand what to do.

3) Identify your papers

Civil service exams are usually identified by number only. You will be assigned a number; you must not put your name on your test papers. Be sure to copy your number correctly. Since more than one exam may be given, copy your exact examination title.

4) Plan your time

Unless you are told that a test is a "speed" or "rate of work" test, speed itself is usually not important. Time enough to answer all the questions will be provided, but this does not mean that you have all day. An overall time limit has been set. Divide the total time (in minutes) by the number of questions to determine the approximate time you have for each question.

5) Do not linger over difficult questions

If you come across a difficult question, mark it with a paper clip (useful to have along) and come back to it when you have been through the booklet. One caution if you do this – be sure to skip a number on your answer sheet as well. Check often to be sure that you have not lost your place and that you are marking in the row numbered the same as the question you are answering.

6) Read the questions

Be sure you know what the question asks! Many capable people are unsuccessful because they failed to *read* the questions correctly.

7) Answer all questions

Unless you have been instructed that a penalty will be deducted for incorrect answers, it is better to guess than to omit a question.

8) Speed tests

It is often better NOT to guess on speed tests. It has been found that on timed tests people are tempted to spend the last few seconds before time is called in marking answers at random – without even reading them – in the hope of picking up a few extra points. To discourage this practice, the instructions may warn you that your score will be "corrected" for guessing. That is, a penalty will be applied. The incorrect answers will be deducted from the correct ones, or some other penalty formula will be used.

9) Review your answers

If you finish before time is called, go back to the questions you guessed or omitted to give them further thought. Review other answers if you have time.

10) Return your test materials

If you are ready to leave before others have finished or time is called, take ALL your materials to the monitor and leave quietly. Never take any test material with you. The monitor can discover whose papers are not complete, and taking a test booklet may be grounds for disqualification.

VIII. EXAMINATION TECHNIQUES

1) Read the general instructions carefully. These are usually printed on the first page of the exam booklet. As a rule, these instructions refer to the timing of the examination; the fact that you should not start work until the signal and must stop work at a signal, etc. If there are any *special* instructions, such as a choice of questions to be answered, make sure that you note this instruction carefully.

2) When you are ready to start work on the examination, that is as soon as the signal has been given, read the instructions to each question booklet, underline any key words or phrases, such as *least, best, outline, describe* and the like. In this way you will tend to answer as requested rather than discover on reviewing your paper that you *listed without describing*, that you selected the *worst* choice rather than the *best* choice, etc.

3) If the examination is of the objective or multiple-choice type – that is, each question will also give a series of possible answers: A, B, C or D, and you are called upon to select the best answer and write the letter next to that answer on your answer paper – it is advisable to start answering each question in turn. There may be anywhere from 50 to 100 such questions in the three or four hours allotted and you can see how much time would be taken if you read through all the questions before beginning to answer any. Furthermore, if you come across a question or group of questions which you know would be difficult to answer, it would undoubtedly affect your handling of all the other questions.

4) If the examination is of the essay type and contains but a few questions, it is a moot point as to whether you should read all the questions before starting to answer any one. Of course, if you are given a choice – say five out of seven and the like – then it is essential to read all the questions so you can eliminate the two that are most difficult. If, however, you are asked to answer all the questions, there may be danger in trying to answer the easiest one first because you may find that you will spend too much time on it. The best technique is to answer the first question, then proceed to the second, etc.

5) Time your answers. Before the exam begins, write down the time it started, then add the time allowed for the examination and write down the time it must be completed, then divide the time available somewhat as follows:
    - If 3-1/2 hours are allowed, that would be 210 minutes. If you have 80 objective-type questions, that would be an average of 2-1/2 minutes per question. Allow yourself no more than 2 minutes per question, or a total of 160 minutes, which will permit about 50 minutes to review.
    - If for the time allotment of 210 minutes there are 7 essay questions to answer, that would average about 30 minutes a question. Give yourself only 25 minutes per question so that you have about 35 minutes to review.

6) The most important instruction is to *read each question* and make sure you know what is wanted. The second most important instruction is to *time yourself properly* so that you answer every question. The third most important instruction is to *answer every question*. Guess if you have to but include something for each question. Remember that you will receive no credit for a blank and will probably receive some credit if you write something in answer to an essay question. If you guess a letter – say "B" for a multiple-choice question – you may have guessed right. If you leave a blank as an answer to a multiple-choice question, the examiners may respect your feelings but it will not add a point to your score. Some exams may penalize you for wrong answers, so in such cases *only*, you may not want to guess unless you have some basis for your answer.

7) Suggestions
    a. Objective-type questions
        1. Examine the question booklet for proper sequence of pages and questions
        2. Read all instructions carefully
        3. Skip any question which seems too difficult; return to it after all other questions have been answered
        4. Apportion your time properly; do not spend too much time on any single question or group of questions

5. Note and underline key words – *all, most, fewest, least, best, worst, same, opposite*, etc.
6. Pay particular attention to negatives
7. Note unusual option, e.g., unduly long, short, complex, different or similar in content to the body of the question
8. Observe the use of "hedging" words – *probably, may, most likely*, etc.
9. Make sure that your answer is put next to the same number as the question
10. Do not second-guess unless you have good reason to believe the second answer is definitely more correct
11. Cross out original answer if you decide another answer is more accurate; do not erase until you are ready to hand your paper in
12. Answer all questions; guess unless instructed otherwise
13. Leave time for review

b. Essay questions
1. Read each question carefully
2. Determine exactly what is wanted. Underline key words or phrases.
3. Decide on outline or paragraph answer
4. Include many different points and elements unless asked to develop any one or two points or elements
5. Show impartiality by giving pros and cons unless directed to select one side only
6. Make and write down any assumptions you find necessary to answer the questions
7. Watch your English, grammar, punctuation and choice of words
8. Time your answers; don't crowd material

8) Answering the essay question

Most essay questions can be answered by framing the specific response around several key words or ideas. Here are a few such key words or ideas:

M's: manpower, materials, methods, money, management
P's: purpose, program, policy, plan, procedure, practice, problems, pitfalls, personnel, public relations

a. Six basic steps in handling problems:
1. Preliminary plan and background development
2. Collect information, data and facts
3. Analyze and interpret information, data and facts
4. Analyze and develop solutions as well as make recommendations
5. Prepare report and sell recommendations
6. Install recommendations and follow up effectiveness

b. Pitfalls to avoid
1. *Taking things for granted* – A statement of the situation does not necessarily imply that each of the elements is necessarily true; for example, a complaint may be invalid and biased so that all that can be taken for granted is that a complaint has been registered

2. *Considering only one side of a situation* – Wherever possible, indicate several alternatives and then point out the reasons you selected the best one
3. *Failing to indicate follow up* – Whenever your answer indicates action on your part, make certain that you will take proper follow-up action to see how successful your recommendations, procedures or actions turn out to be
4. *Taking too long in answering any single question* – Remember to time your answers properly

IX. AFTER THE TEST

Scoring procedures differ in detail among civil service jurisdictions although the general principles are the same. Whether the papers are hand-scored or graded by machine we have described, they are nearly always graded by number. That is, the person who marks the paper knows only the number – never the name – of the applicant. Not until all the papers have been graded will they be matched with names. If other tests, such as training and experience or oral interview ratings have been given, scores will be combined. Different parts of the examination usually have different weights. For example, the written test might count 60 percent of the final grade, and a rating of training and experience 40 percent. In many jurisdictions, veterans will have a certain number of points added to their grades.

After the final grade has been determined, the names are placed in grade order and an eligible list is established. There are various methods for resolving ties between those who get the same final grade – probably the most common is to place first the name of the person whose application was received first. Job offers are made from the eligible list in the order the names appear on it. You will be notified of your grade and your rank as soon as all these computations have been made. This will be done as rapidly as possible.

People who are found to meet the requirements in the announcement are called "eligibles." Their names are put on a list of eligible candidates. An eligible's chances of getting a job depend on how high he stands on this list and how fast agencies are filling jobs from the list.

When a job is to be filled from a list of eligibles, the agency asks for the names of people on the list of eligibles for that job. When the civil service commission receives this request, it sends to the agency the names of the three people highest on this list. Or, if the job to be filled has specialized requirements, the office sends the agency the names of the top three persons who meet these requirements from the general list.

The appointing officer makes a choice from among the three people whose names were sent to him. If the selected person accepts the appointment, the names of the others are put back on the list to be considered for future openings.

That is the rule in hiring from all kinds of eligible lists, whether they are for typist, carpenter, chemist, or something else. For every vacancy, the appointing officer has his choice of any one of the top three eligibles on the list. This explains why the person whose name is on top of the list sometimes does not get an appointment when some of the persons lower on the list do. If the appointing officer chooses the second or third eligible, the No. 1 eligible does not get a job at once, but stays on the list until he is appointed or the list is terminated.

X. HOW TO PASS THE INTERVIEW TEST

The examination for which you applied requires an oral interview test. You have already taken the written test and you are now being called for the interview test – the final part of the formal examination.

You may think that it is not possible to prepare for an interview test and that there are no procedures to follow during an interview. Our purpose is to point out some things you can do in advance that will help you and some good rules to follow and pitfalls to avoid while you are being interviewed.

What is an interview supposed to test?

The written examination is designed to test the technical knowledge and competence of the candidate; the oral is designed to evaluate intangible qualities, not readily measured otherwise, and to establish a list showing the relative fitness of each candidate – as measured against his competitors – for the position sought. Scoring is not on the basis of "right" and "wrong," but on a sliding scale of values ranging from "not passable" to "outstanding." As a matter of fact, it is possible to achieve a relatively low score without a single "incorrect" answer because of evident weakness in the qualities being measured.

Occasionally, an examination may consist entirely of an oral test – either an individual or a group oral. In such cases, information is sought concerning the technical knowledges and abilities of the candidate, since there has been no written examination for this purpose. More commonly, however, an oral test is used to supplement a written examination.

Who conducts interviews?

The composition of oral boards varies among different jurisdictions. In nearly all, a representative of the personnel department serves as chairman. One of the members of the board may be a representative of the department in which the candidate would work. In some cases, "outside experts" are used, and, frequently, a businessman or some other representative of the general public is asked to serve. Labor and management or other special groups may be represented. The aim is to secure the services of experts in the appropriate field.

However the board is composed, it is a good idea (and not at all improper or unethical) to ascertain in advance of the interview who the members are and what groups they represent. When you are introduced to them, you will have some idea of their backgrounds and interests, and at least you will not stutter and stammer over their names.

What should be done before the interview?

While knowledge about the board members is useful and takes some of the surprise element out of the interview, there is other preparation which is more substantive. It *is* possible to prepare for an oral interview – in several ways:

1) Keep a copy of your application and review it carefully before the interview

This may be the only document before the oral board, and the starting point of the interview. Know what education and experience you have listed there, and the sequence and dates of all of it. Sometimes the board will ask you to review the highlights of your experience for them; you should not have to hem and haw doing it.

2) Study the class specification and the examination announcement

Usually, the oral board has one or both of these to guide them. The qualities, characteristics or knowledges required by the position sought are stated in these documents. They offer valuable clues as to the nature of the oral interview. For example, if the job involves supervisory responsibilities, the announcement will usually indicate that knowledge of modern supervisory methods and the qualifications of the candidate as a supervisor will be tested. If so, you can expect such questions, frequently in the form of a hypothetical situation which you are expected to solve. NEVER go into an oral without knowledge of the duties and responsibilities of the job you seek.

3) Think through each qualification required

Try to visualize the kind of questions you would ask if you were a board member. How well could you answer them? Try especially to appraise your own knowledge and background in each area, *measured against the job sought*, and identify any areas in which you are weak. Be critical and realistic – do not flatter yourself.

4) Do some general reading in areas in which you feel you may be weak

For example, if the job involves supervision and your past experience has NOT, some general reading in supervisory methods and practices, particularly in the field of human relations, might be useful. Do NOT study agency procedures or detailed manuals. The oral board will be testing your understanding and capacity, not your memory.

5) Get a good night's sleep and watch your general health and mental attitude

You will want a clear head at the interview. Take care of a cold or any other minor ailment, and of course, no hangovers.

What should be done on the day of the interview?

Now comes the day of the interview itself. Give yourself plenty of time to get there. Plan to arrive somewhat ahead of the scheduled time, particularly if your appointment is in the fore part of the day. If a previous candidate fails to appear, the board might be ready for you a bit early. By early afternoon an oral board is almost invariably behind schedule if there are many candidates, and you may have to wait. Take along a book or magazine to read, or your application to review, but leave any extraneous material in the waiting room when you go in for your interview. In any event, relax and compose yourself.

The matter of dress is important. The board is forming impressions about you – from your experience, your manners, your attitude, and your appearance. Give your personal appearance careful attention. Dress your best, but not your flashiest. Choose conservative, appropriate clothing, and be sure it is immaculate. This is a business interview, and your appearance should indicate that you regard it as such. Besides, being well groomed and properly dressed will help boost your confidence.

Sooner or later, someone will call your name and escort you into the interview room. *This is it.* From here on you are on your own. It is too late for any more preparation. But remember, you asked for this opportunity to prove your fitness, and you are here because your request was granted.

What happens when you go in?

The usual sequence of events will be as follows: The clerk (who is often the board stenographer) will introduce you to the chairman of the oral board, who will introduce you to the other members of the board. Acknowledge the introductions before you sit down. Do not be surprised if you find a microphone facing you or a stenotypist sitting by. Oral interviews are usually recorded in the event of an appeal or other review.

Usually the chairman of the board will open the interview by reviewing the highlights of your education and work experience from your application – primarily for the benefit of the other members of the board, as well as to get the material into the record. Do not interrupt or comment unless there is an error or significant misinterpretation; if that is the case, do not hesitate. But do not quibble about insignificant matters. Also, he will usually ask you some question about your education, experience or your present job – partly to get you to start talking and to establish the interviewing "rapport." He may start the actual questioning, or turn it over to one of the other members. Frequently, each member undertakes the questioning on a particular area, one in which he is perhaps most competent, so you can expect each member to participate in the examination. Because time is limited, you may also expect some rather abrupt switches in the direction the questioning takes, so do not be upset by it. Normally, a board member will not pursue a single line of questioning unless he discovers a particular strength or weakness.

After each member has participated, the chairman will usually ask whether any member has any further questions, then will ask you if you have anything you wish to add. Unless you are expecting this question, it may floor you. Worse, it may start you off on an extended, extemporaneous speech. The board is not usually seeking more information. The question is principally to offer you a last opportunity to present further qualifications or to indicate that you have nothing to add. So, if you feel that a significant qualification or characteristic has been overlooked, it is proper to point it out in a sentence or so. Do not compliment the board on the thoroughness of their examination – they have been sketchy, and you know it. If you wish, merely say, "No thank you, I have nothing further to add." This is a point where you can "talk yourself out" of a good impression or fail to present an important bit of information. Remember, *you close the interview yourself.*

The chairman will then say, "That is all, Mr. _____, thank you." Do not be startled; the interview is over, and quicker than you think. Thank him, gather your belongings and take your leave. Save your sigh of relief for the other side of the door.

How to put your best foot forward

Throughout this entire process, you may feel that the board individually and collectively is trying to pierce your defenses, seek out your hidden weaknesses and embarrass and confuse you. Actually, this is not true. They are obliged to make an appraisal of your qualifications for the job you are seeking, and they want to see you in your best light. Remember, they must interview all candidates and a non-cooperative candidate may become a failure in spite of their best efforts to bring out his qualifications. Here are 15 suggestions that will help you:

1) Be natural – Keep your attitude confident, not cocky

If you are not confident that you can do the job, do not expect the board to be. Do not apologize for your weaknesses, try to bring out your strong points. The board is interested in a positive, not negative, presentation. Cockiness will antagonize any board member and make him wonder if you are covering up a weakness by a false show of strength.

2) Get comfortable, but don't lounge or sprawl

Sit erectly but not stiffly. A careless posture may lead the board to conclude that you are careless in other things, or at least that you are not impressed by the importance of the occasion. Either conclusion is natural, even if incorrect. Do not fuss with your clothing, a pencil or an ashtray. Your hands may occasionally be useful to emphasize a point; do not let them become a point of distraction.

3) Do not wisecrack or make small talk

This is a serious situation, and your attitude should show that you consider it as such. Further, the time of the board is limited – they do not want to waste it, and neither should you.

4) Do not exaggerate your experience or abilities
In the first place, from information in the application or other interviews and sources, the board may know more about you than you think. Secondly, you probably will not get away with it. An experienced board is rather adept at spotting such a situation, so do not take the chance.

5) If you know a board member, do not make a point of it, yet do not hide it
Certainly you are not fooling him, and probably not the other members of the board. Do not try to take advantage of your acquaintanceship – it will probably do you little good.

6) Do not dominate the interview
Let the board do that. They will give you the clues – do not assume that you have to do all the talking. Realize that the board has a number of questions to ask you, and do not try to take up all the interview time by showing off your extensive knowledge of the answer to the first one.

7) Be attentive
You only have 20 minutes or so, and you should keep your attention at its sharpest throughout. When a member is addressing a problem or question to you, give him your undivided attention. Address your reply principally to him, but do not exclude the other board members.

8) Do not interrupt
A board member may be stating a problem for you to analyze. He will ask you a question when the time comes. Let him state the problem, and wait for the question.

9) Make sure you understand the question
Do not try to answer until you are sure what the question is. If it is not clear, restate it in your own words or ask the board member to clarify it for you. However, do not haggle about minor elements.

10) Reply promptly but not hastily
A common entry on oral board rating sheets is "candidate responded readily," or "candidate hesitated in replies." Respond as promptly and quickly as you can, but do not jump to a hasty, ill-considered answer.

11) Do not be peremptory in your answers
A brief answer is proper – but do not fire your answer back. That is a losing game from your point of view. The board member can probably ask questions much faster than you can answer them.

12) Do not try to create the answer you think the board member wants
He is interested in what kind of mind you have and how it works – not in playing games. Furthermore, he can usually spot this practice and will actually grade you down on it.

13) Do not switch sides in your reply merely to agree with a board member
Frequently, a member will take a contrary position merely to draw you out and to see if you are willing and able to defend your point of view. Do not start a debate, yet do not surrender a good position. If a position is worth taking, it is worth defending.

14) Do not be afraid to admit an error in judgment if you are shown to be wrong

The board knows that you are forced to reply without any opportunity for careful consideration. Your answer may be demonstrably wrong. If so, admit it and get on with the interview.

15) Do not dwell at length on your present job

The opening question may relate to your present assignment. Answer the question but do not go into an extended discussion. You are being examined for a *new* job, not your present one. As a matter of fact, try to phrase ALL your answers in terms of the job for which you are being examined.

Basis of Rating

Probably you will forget most of these "do's" and "don'ts" when you walk into the oral interview room. Even remembering them all will not ensure you a passing grade. Perhaps you did not have the qualifications in the first place. But remembering them will help you to put your best foot forward, without treading on the toes of the board members.

Rumor and popular opinion to the contrary notwithstanding, an oral board wants you to make the best appearance possible. They know you are under pressure – but they also want to see how you respond to it as a guide to what your reaction would be under the pressures of the job you seek. They will be influenced by the degree of poise you display, the personal traits you show and the manner in which you respond.

ABOUT THIS BOOK

This book contains tests divided into Examination Sections. Go through each test, answering every question in the margin. We have also attached a sample answer sheet at the back of the book that can be removed and used. At the end of each test look at the answer key and check your answers. On the ones you got wrong, look at the right answer choice and learn. Do not fill in the answers first. Do not memorize the questions and answers, but understand the answer and principles involved. On your test, the questions will likely be different from the samples. Questions are changed and new ones added. If you understand these past questions you should have success with any changes that arise. Tests may consist of several types of questions. We have additional books on each subject should more study be advisable or necessary for you. Finally, the more you study, the better prepared you will be. This book is intended to be the last thing you study before you walk into the examination room. Prior study of relevant texts is also recommended. NLC publishes some of these in our Fundamental Series. Knowledge and good sense are important factors in passing your exam. Good luck also helps. So now study this Passbook, absorb the material contained within and take that knowledge into the examination. Then do your best to pass that exam.

EXAMINATION SECTION

REPORT WRITING

EXAMINATION SECTION

TEST 1

DIRECTIONS: Each question or incomplete statement is followed by several suggested answers or completions. Select the one that BEST answers the question or completes the statement. *PRINT THE LETTER OF THE CORRECT ANSWER IN THE SPACE AT THE RIGHT.*

Questions 1-4.

DIRECTIONS: Answer Questions 1 through 4 on the basis of the following report which was prepared by a supervisor for inclusion in his agency's annual report.

Line #
1 On Oct. 13, I was assigned to study the salaries paid.
2 to clerical employees in various titles by the city and by
3 private industry in the area.
4 In order to get the data I needed, I called Mr. Johnson at
5 the Bureau of the Budget and the payroll officers at X Corp.—
6 a brokerage house, Y Co. —an insurance company, and Z Inc. —
7 a publishing firm. None of them was available and I had to call
8 all of them again the next day.
9 When I finally got the information I needed, I drew up a
10 chart, which is attached. Note that not all of the companies I
11 contacted employed people at all the different levels used in the
12 city service.
13 The conclusions I draw from analyzing this information is
14 as follows: The city's entry-level salary is about average for
15 the region; middle-level salaries are generally higher in the
16 city government plan than in private industry; but salaries at the
17 highest levels in private industry are better than city em-
18 ployees' pay.

1. Which of the following criticisms about the style in which this report is written is MOST valid?
   A. It is too informal.
   B. It is too concise.
   C. It is too choppy.
   D. The syntax is too complex.

   1._____

2. Judging from the statements made in the report, the method followed by this employee in performing his research was
   A. *good*; he contacted a representative sample of businesses in the area
   B. *poor*; he should have drawn more definite conclusions
   C. *good*; he was persistent in collecting information
   D. *poor*; he did not make a thorough study

   2._____

3. One sentence in this report contains a grammatical error. This sentence begins on line number
   A. 4　　　　B. 7　　　　C. 10　　　　D. 14

4. The type of information given in this report which should be presented in footnotes or in an appendix is the
   A. purpose of the study
   B. specifics about the businesses contacted
   C. reference to the chart
   D. conclusions drawn by the author

5. The use of a graph to show statistical data in a report is SUPERIOR to a table because it
   A. features approximations
   B. emphasizes facts and relationships more dramatically
   C. presents data more accurately
   D. is easily understood by the average reader

6. Of the following, the degree of formality required of a written report in tone is MOST likely to depend on the
   A. subject matter of the report
   B. frequency of its occurrence
   C. amount of time available for its preparation
   D. audience for whom the report is intended

7. Of the following, a distinguishing characteristic of a written report intended for the head of your agency as compared to a report prepared for a lower-echelon staff member is that the report for the agency head should USUALLY include
   A. considerably more detail, especially statistical data
   B. the essential details in an abbreviated form
   C. all available source material
   D. an annotated bibliography

8. Assume that you are asked to write a lengthy report for use by the administrator of your agency, the subject of which is "The Impact of Proposed New Data Processing Operation on Line Personnel" in your agency. You decide that the *most* appropriate type of report for you to prepare is an analytical report, including recommendations.
   The MAIN reason for your decision is that
   A. the subject of the report is extremely complex
   B. large sums of money are involved
   C. the report is being prepared for the administrator
   D. you intend to include charts and graphs

9. Assume that you are preparing a report based on a survey dealing with the attitudes of employees in Division X regarding proposed new changes in compensating employees for working overtime. Three percent of the respondents to the survey voluntarily offer an unfavorable opinion on the method of assigning overtime work, a question not specifically asked of the employees.
   On the basis of this information, the MOST appropriate and significant of the following comments for you to make in the report with regard to employees' attitudes on assigning overtime work is that
   A. an insignificant percentage of employees dislike the method of assigning overtime work
   B. three percent of the employees in Division X dislike the method of assigning overtime work
   C. three percent of the sample selected for the survey voiced an unfavorable opinion on the method of assigning overtime work
   D. some employees voluntarily voiced negative feelings about the method of assigning overtime work, making it impossible to determine the extent of this attitude

10. A supervisor should be able to prepare a report that is well-written and unambiguous.
    Of the following sentences that might appear in a report, select the one which communicates MOST clearly the intent of its author.
    A. When your subordinates speak to a group of people, they should be well-informed.
    B. When he asked him to leave, SanMan King told him that he would refuse the request.
    C. Because he is a good worker, Foreman Jefferson assigned Assistant Foreman D'Agostino to replace him.
    D. Each of us is responsible for the actions of our subordinates.

11. In some reports, especially longer ones, a list of the resources (books, papers, magazines, etc.) used to prepare it is included. This list is called the
    A. accreditation   B. bibliography
    C. summary   D. glossary

12. Reports are usually divided into several sections, some of which are more necessary than others.
    Of the following, the section which is ABSOLUTELY necessary to include in a report is
    A. a table of contents   B. the body
    C. an index   D. a bibliography

13. Suppose you are writing a report on an interview you have just completed with a particularly hostile applicant.
    Which of the following BEST describes what you should include in this report?
    A. What you think caused the applicant's hostile attitude during the interview
    B. Specific examples of the applicant's hostile remarks and behavior
    C. The relevant information uncovered during the interview
    D. A recommendation that the applicant's request be denied because of his hostility

14. When including recommendations in a report to your supervisor, which of the following is MOST important for you to do?
    A. Provide several alternative courses of action for each recommendation
    B. First present the supporting evidence, then the recommendations
    C. First present the recommendations, then the supporting evidence
    D. Make sure the recommendations arise logically out of the information in the report

15. It is often necessary that the writer of a report present facts and sufficient arguments to gain acceptance of the points, conclusions, or recommendations set forth in the report.
    Of the following, the LEAST advisable step to take in organizing a report, when such argumentation is the important factor, is a(n)
    A. elaborate expression of personal belief
    B. businesslike discussion of the problem as a whole
    C. orderly arrangement of convincing data
    D. reasonable explanation of the primary issues

16. In some types of reports, visual aids add interest, meaning, and support. They also provide an essential means of effectively communicating the message of the report.
    Of the following, the selection of the suitable visual aids to use with a report is LEAST dependent on the
    A. nature and scope of the report
    B. way in which the aid is to be used
    C. aid used in other reports
    D. prospective readers of the report

17. Visual aids used in a report may be placed either in the text material or in the appendix.
    Deciding where to put a chart, table, or any such aid should depend on the
    A. title of the report   B. purpose of the visual aid
    C. title of the visual aid   D. length of the report

18. A report is often revised several times before final preparation and distribution in an effort to make certain the report meets the needs of the situation for which it is designed.
    Which of the following is the BEST way for the author to be sure that a report covers the areas he intended?

A. Obtain a coworker's opinion
B. Compare it with a content checklist
C. Test it on a subordinate
D. Check his bibliography

19. In which of the following situations is an oral report preferable to a written report? When a(n)
    A. recommendation is being made for a future plan of action
    B. department head requests immediate information
    C. long-standing policy change is made
    D. analysis of complicated statistical data is involved

20. When an applicant is approved, the supervisor must fill in standard forms with certain information.
    The GREATEST advantage of using standard forms in this situation rather than having the supervisor write the report as he sees fit is that
    A. the report can be acted on quickly
    B. the report can be written without directions from a supervisor
    C. needed information is less likely to be left out of the report
    D. information that is written up this way is more likely to be verified

21. Assume that it is part of your job to prepare a monthly report for your unit head that eventually goes to the director. The report contains information on the number of applicants you have interviewed that have been approved and the number of applicants you have interviewed that have been turned down.
    Errors on such reports are serious because
    A. you are expected to be able to prove how many applicants you have interviewed each month
    B. accurate statistics are needed for effective management of the department
    C. they may not be discovered before the report is transmitted to the director
    D. they may result in loss to the applicants left out of the report

22. The frequency with which job reports are submitted should depend MAINLY on
    A. how comprehensive the report has to be
    B. the amount of information in the report
    C. the availability of an experienced man to write the report
    D. the importance of changes in the information included in the report

23. The CHIEF purpose in preparing an outline for a report is usually to insure that
    A. the report will be grammatically correct
    B. every point will be given equal emphasis
    C. principal and secondary points will be properly integrated
    D. the language of the report will be of the same level and include the same technical terms

24. The MAIN reason for requiring written job reports is to
     A. avoid the necessity of oral orders
     B. develop better methods of doing the work
     C. provide a permanent record of what was done
     D. increase the amount of work that can be done

24.____

25. Assume you are recommending in a report to your supervisor that a radical change in a standard maintenance procedure should be adopted.
    Of the following, the MOST important information to be included in this report is
     A. a list of the reasons for making this change
     B. the names of others who favor the change
     C. a complete description of the present procedure
     D. amount of training time needed for the new procedure

25.____

KEY (CORRECT ANSWERS)

1.	A		11.	B
2.	D		12.	B
3.	D		13.	C
4.	B		14.	D
5.	B		15.	A
6.	D		16.	C
7.	B		17.	B
8.	A		18.	B
9.	D		19.	B
10.	D		20.	C

21. B
22. D
23. C
24. C
25. A

TEST 2

DIRECTIONS: Each question or incomplete statement is followed by several suggested answers or completions. Select the one that BEST answers the question or completes the statement. *PRINT THE LETTER OF THE CORRECT ANSWER IN THE SPACE AT THE RIGHT.*

1. It is often necessary that the writer of a report present facts and sufficient arguments to gain acceptance of the points, conclusions, or recommendations set forth in the report.
   Of the following, the LEAST advisable step to take in organizing a report, when such argumentation is the important factor, is a(n)
   A. elaborate expression of personal belief
   B. businesslike discussion of the problem as a whole
   C. orderly arrangement of convincing data
   D. reasonable explanation of the primary issues

2. Of the following, the factor which is generally considered to be LEAST characteristic of a good control report is that it
   A. stresses performance that adheres to standard rather than emphasizing the exception
   B. supplies information intended to serve as the basis for corrective action
   C. provides feedback for the planning process
   D. includes data that reflect trends as well as current status

3. An administrative assistant has been asked by his superior to write a concise, factual report with objective conclusions and recommendations based on facts assembled by other researchers.
   Of the following factors, the administrative assistant should give LEAST consideration to
   A. the educational level of the person or persons for whom the report is being prepared
   B. the use to be made of the report
   C. the complexity of the problem
   D. his own feelings about the importance of the problem

4. When making a written report, it is often recommended that the findings or conclusions be presented near the beginning of the report.
   Of the following, the MOST important reason for doing this is that it
   A. facilitates organizing the material clearly
   B. assures that all the topics will be covered
   C. avoids unnecessary repetition of ideas
   D. prepares the reader for the facts that will follow

5. You have been asked to write a report on methods of hiring and training new employees. Your report is going to be about ten pages long.
   For the convenience of your readers, a brief summary of your findings should
   A. appear at the beginning of your report
   B. be appended to the report as a postscript
   C. be circulated in a separate memo
   D. be inserted in tabular form in the middle of your report

5.____

6. In preparing a report, the MAIN reason for writing an outline is usually to
   A. help organize thoughts in a logical sequence
   B. provide a guide for the typing of the report
   C. allow the ultimate user to review the report in advance
   D. ensure that the report is being prepared on schedule

6.____

7. The one of the following which is MOST appropriate as a reason for including footnotes in a report is to
   A. correct capitalization   B. delete passages
   C. improve punctuation   D. cite references

7.____

8. A completed formal report may contain all of the following EXCEPT
   A. a synopsis   B. a preface
   C. marginal notes   D. bibliographical references

8.____

9. Of the following, the MAIN use of proofreaders' marks is to
   A. explain corrections to be made
   B. indicate that a manuscript has been read and approved
   C. let the reader know who proofread the report
   D. indicate the format of the report

9.____

10. Informative, readable, and concise reports have been found to observe the following rules:
    Rule I.   Keep the report short and easy to understand
    Rule II. Vary the length of sentences.
    Rule III. Vary the style of sentences so that, for example, they are not all just subject-verb, subject-verb.
    Consider this hospital laboratory report: The experiment was started in January. The apparatus was put together in six weeks. At that time, the synthesizing process was begun. The synthetic chemicals were separated. Then they were used in tests on patients.
    Which one of the following choices MOST accurately classifies the above rules into those which are violated by this report ad those which are not?
    A. II is violated, but I and III are not.
    B. III is violated, but I and II are not.
    C. II and III are violated, but I is not.
    D. I, II, and III are violated,

10.____

Questions 11-13.

DIRECTIONS: Questions 11 through 13 are based on the following example of a report. The report consists of eight numbered sentences, some of which are not consistent with the principles of good report writing.

(1) I interviewed Mrs. Loretta Crawford in Room 424 of County Hospital. (2) She had collapsed on the street and been brought into emergency. (3) She is an attractive woman with many friends judging by the cards she had received. (4) She did not know what her husband's last job had been, or what their present income was. (5) The first thing that Mrs. Crawford said was that she had never worked and that her husband was presently unemployed. (6) She did not know if they had any medical coverage or if they could pay the bill. (7) She said that her husband could not be reached by telephone but that he would be in to see her that afternoon. (8) I left word at the nursing station to be called when he arrived.

11. A good report should be arranged in logical order.
    Which of the following sentences from the report does NOT appear in its proper sequence in the report?
    A. 1   B. 4   C. 7   D. 8

12. Only material that is relevant to the main thought of a report should be included. Which of the following sentences from the report contains material which is LEAST relevant to this report? Sentence
    A. 3   B. 4   C. 6   D. 8

13. Reports should include all essential information.
    Of the following, the MOST important fact that is missing from this report is:
    A. Who was involved in the interview
    B. What was discovered at the interview
    C. When the interview took place
    D. Where the interview took place

Questions 14-15.

DIRECTIONS: Each of Questions 14 and 15 consists of four numbered sentences which constitute a paragraph in a report. They are not in the right order. Choose the numbered arrangement appearing after letter A, B, C, or D which is MOST logical and which BEST expresses the thought of the paragraph.

14. I.   Congress made the commitment explicit in the Housing Act of 1949, establishing as a national goal the realization of a decent home and suitable environment for every American family.
    II. The result has been that the goal of decent home and suitable environment is still as far distant as ever for the disadvantaged urban family
    III. In spite of this action by Congress, federal housing programs have continued to be fragmented and grossly under-funded.
    IV. The passage of the National Housing Act signaled a new federal commitment to provide housing for the nation's citizens.

The CORRECT answer is:
A. I, IV, III, II   B. IV, I, III, II   C. IV, I, III, II   D. II, IV, I, III

15.
   I. The greater expense does not necessarily involve "exploitation," but it is often perceived as exploitative and unfair by those who are aware of the price differences involved, but unaware of operating costs.
   II. Ghetto residents believe they are "exploited" by local merchants, and evidence substantiates some of these beliefs.
   III. However, stores in low-income areas were more likely to be small independents, which could not achieve the economies available to supermarket chains and were, therefore, more likely to charge higher prices, and the customers were more likely to buy smaller-sized packages which are more expensive per unit of measure.
   IV. A study conducted in one city showed that distinctly higher prices were charged for goods sold in ghetto stores than in other areas.

   The CORRECT answer is:
   A. IV, II, I, III   B. IV, I, III, II   C. II, IV, III, I   D. II, III, IV, I

16. In organizing data to be presented in a formal report, the FIRST of the following steps should be
    A. determining the conclusions to be drawn
    B. establishing the time sequence of the data
    C. sorting and arranging like data into groups
    D. evaluating how consistently the data support the recommendations

17. All reports should be prepared with at least one copy so that
    A. there is one copy for your file
    B. there is a copy for your supervisor
    C. the report can be sent to more than one person
    D. the person getting the report can forward a copy to someone else

18. Before turning in a report of an investigation he has made, a supervisor discovers some additional information he did not include in this report. Whether he rewrites this report to include this additional information should PRIMARILY depend on the
    A. importance of the report itself
    B. number of people who will eventually review this report
    C. established policy covering the subject matter of the report
    D. bearing this new information has on the conclusions of the report

KEY (CORRECT ANSWERS)

1.	A	11.	B
2.	A	12.	A
3.	D	13.	C
4.	D	14.	B
5.	A	15.	C
6.	A	16.	C
7.	D	17.	A
8.	C	18.	D
9.	A		
10.	C		

REPORT WRITING

EXAMINATION SECTION

TEST 1

DIRECTIONS: Each question or incomplete statement is followed by several suggested answers or completions. Select the one that BEST answers the question or completes the statement. *PRINT THE LETTER OF THE CORRECT ANSWER IN THE SPACE AT THE RIGHT.*

Questions 1-3.

DIRECTIONS: Questions 1 to 3 are based on the following example of a report. The report consists of ten numbered sentences, some of which are *not* consistent with the principles of good report writing.

(1) On the evening of February 24, Roscoe and Leroy, two members of the "Red Devils," were entering with a bottle of wine in their hands. (2) It was unusually good wine for these boys to buy, (3) I told them to give me the bottle and they refused, and added that they wouldn't let anyone "put them out." (4) I told them they were entitled to have a good time, but they could not do it the way they wanted; there were certain rules they had to observe. (5) At this point, Roscoe said he had seen me box at camp and suggested that Leroy not accept my offer. (6) Then I said firmly that the admission fee did not give them the authority to tell me what to do. (7) I also told them that, if they thought I would fight them over such a matter, they were sadly mistaken. (8) I added, however, that we could go to the gym right now and settle it another way if they wished. (9) Leroy immediately said that he was sorry, he had not understood the rules, and he did not want his quarter back. (10) On the other hand, they would not give up their bottle either, so they left the premises.

1. Only material that is relevant to the main thought of a report should be included. Which of the following sentences from the report contains material which is LEAST relevant to this report? Sentence
    A. 2   B. 3   C. 8   D. 9

2. A good report should be arranged in logical order. Which of the following sentences from the report does NOT appear in its proper sequence in the report? Sentence
    A. 3   B. 5   C. 7   D. 9

3. Reports should include all essential information. Of the following, the MOST important fact that is *missing* from this report is:
    A. Who was involved in the incident   B. How the incident was resolved
    C. When the incident took place   D. Where the incident took place

4. The MOST serious of the following faults *commonly* found in explanatory reports is
    A. the use of slang terms   B. excessive details
    C. personal bias   D. redundancy

5. In reviewing a report he has prepared to submit to his superiors, a supervisor finds that his paragraphs are a typewritten page long and decides to make some revisions.
Of the following, the MOST important question he should ask about each paragraph is
   A. Are the words too lengthy?
   B. Is the idea under discussion too abstract?
   C. Is more than one central thought being expressed?
   D. Are the sentences too long?

5.____

6. The summary or findings of a long management report intended for the typical manager should, *generally*, appear _____ the report.
   A. at the very beginning of B. at the end of
   C. throughout D. in the middle of

6.____

7. In preparing a report that includes several tables, if not otherwise instructed, the typist should MOST properly include a list of tables
   A. in the introductory part of the report
   B. at the end of each chapter in the body of the report
   C. in the supplementary part of the report as an appendix
   D. in the supplementary part of the report as a part of the index

7.____

8. When typing a preliminary draft of a report, the one of the following which you should *generally* NOT do is to
   A. erase typing errors and deletions rather than "X"ing them out
   B. leave plenty of room at the top, bottom, and sides of each page
   C. make only the number of copies that you are asked to make
   D. type double or triple space

8.____

9. When you determine the methods of emphasis you will use in typing the titles, headings and subheadings of a report, the one of the following which it is MOST important to keep in mind is that
   A. all headings of the same rank should be typed in the same way
   B. all headings should be typed in the single style which is most pleasing to the eye
   C. headings should not take up more than one-third of the page width
   D. only one method should be used for all headings, whatever their rank

9.____

10. The one of the following ways in which inter-office memoranda *differ* from long formal reports is that they, *generally*,
    A. are written as if the reader is familiar with the vocabulary and technical background of the writer
    B. do not have a "subject line" which describes the major topic covered in the text
    C. include a listing of reference materials which support the memo writer's conclusions
    D. require that a letter of transmittal be attached

10.____

11. It is *preferable* to print information on a field report rather than write it out longhand MAINLY because
    A. printing takes less time to write than writing long hand
    B. printing is usually easier to read than longhand writing
    C. longhand writing on field reports is not acceptable in court cases
    D. printing occupies less space on a report than longhand writing

12. Of the following characteristics of a written report, the one that is MOST important is its
    A. length   B. accuracy   C. organization   D. grammar

13. A written report to your superior contains many spelling errors.
    Of the following statements relating to spelling errors, the one that is MOST NEARLY correct is that
    A. this is unimportant as long as the meaning of the report is clear
    B. readers of the report will ignore the many spelling errors
    C. readers of the report will get a poor opinion of the writer of the report
    D. spelling errors are unimportant as long as the grammar is correct

14. Written reports to your superior should have the same general arrangement and layout.
    The BEST reason for this requirement is that the
    A. report will be more accurate
    B. report will be more complete
    C. person who reads the report will know what the subject of the report is
    D. person who reads the report will know where to look for information in the report

15. The first paragraph of a report usually contains detailed information on the subject of the report.
    Of the following, the BEST reason for this requirement is to enable the
    A. reader to quickly find the subject of the report
    B. typist to immediately determine the subject of the report so that she will understand what she is typing
    C. clerk to determine to whom copies of the report will be needed
    D. typist to quickly determine how many copies of the report will be needed

16. Of the following statements concerning reports, the one which is LEAST valid is:
    A. A case report should contain factual material to support conclusions made
    B. An extremely detailed report may be of less value than a brief report giving the essential facts
    C. Highly technical language should be avoided as far as possible in preparing a report to be used at a court trial
    D. The position of the important facts in a report does not influence the emphasis placed on them by the reader

17. Suppose that you realize that you have made an error in a report that has been forwarded to another unit. You know that this error is not likely to be discovered for some time.
Of the following, the MOST advisable course of action for you to take is to
   A. approach the supervisor of the other unit on an informal basis, and ask him to correct the error
   B. say nothing about it since most likely one error will not invalidate the entire report
   C. tell your supervisor immediately that you have made an error so that it may be corrected, if necessary
   D. wait until the error is discovered and then admit that you had made it

18. In a report, words in a sentence must be arranged properly to make sure that the intended meaning of the sentence is clear.
The sentence below that does NOT make sense because a clause has been separated from the word on which its meaning depends is:
   A. To be a good writer, clarity is necessary.
   B. To be a good writer, you must write clearly.
   C. You must write clearly to be a good writer.
   D. Clarity is necessary to good writing.

19. The use of a graph to show statistical data in a report is *superior* to a table because it
   A. emphasizes approximations
   B. emphasizes facts and relationships more dramatically
   C. presents data more accurately
   D. is easily understood by the average reader

20. Of the following, the degree of formality required of a written report is, MOST likely to depend on the
   A. subject matter of the report
   B. frequency of its occurrence
   C. amount of time available for its preparation
   D. audience for whom the report is intended

Questions 21-25.

DIRECTIONS: Questions 21 through 25 consist of sets of four sentences lettered A, B, C, and D. For each question, choose the sentence which is grammatically and stylistically MOST appropriate for use in a formal written report.

21. A. It is recommended, therefore, that the impasse panel hearings are to be convened on September 30.
    B. It is therefore recommended that the impasse panel hearings be convened on September 30.
    C. Therefore, it is recommended to convene the impasse panel hearings on September 30.
    D. It is recommended that the impasse panel hearings therefore should be convened on September 30.

22. A. Penalties have been assessed for violating the Taylor Law by several unions.   22.____
    B. When they violated provisions of the Taylor Law, several unions were later penalized.
    C. Several unions have been penalized for violating provisions of the Taylor Law.
    D. Several unions' violating provisions of the Taylor Law resulted in them being penalized.

23. A. The number of disputes settled through mediation has increased significantly over the past two years.   23.____
    B. The number of disputes settled through mediation are increasing significantly over two-year periods.
    C. Over the past two years, through mediation, the number of disputes settled increased significantly.
    D. There is a significant increase over the past two years of the number of disputes settled through mediation.

24. A. The union members will vote to determine if the contract is to be approved.   24.____
    B. It is not yet known whether the union members will ratify the proposed contract.
    C. When the union members vote, that will determine the new contract.
    D. Whether the union members will ratify the proposed contract, it is not yet known.

25. A. The parties agreed to an increase in fringe benefits in return for greater work productivity.   25.____
    B. Greater productivity was agreed to be provided in return for increased fringe benefits.
    C. Productivity and fringe benefits are interrelated; the higher the former, the more the latter grows.
    D. The contract now provides that the amount of fringe benefits will depend upon the level of output by the workers.

KEY (CORRECT ANSWERS)

1.	A	11.	B
2.	B	12.	B
3.	D	13.	C
4.	C	14.	D
5.	C	15.	A
6.	A	16.	D
7.	A	17.	C
8.	A	18.	A
9.	A	19.	B
10.	A	20.	D

21. B
22. C
23. A
24. B
25. A

TEST 2

DIRECTIONS: Each question or incomplete statement is followed by several suggested answers or completions. Select the one that BEST answers the question or completes the statement. *PRINT THE LETTER OF THE CORRECT ANSWER IN THE SPACE AT THE RIGHT.*

Questions 1-4.

DIRECTIONS: Questions 1 through 4 are to be answered on the basis of the following report which was prepared by a supervisor for inclusion in his agency's annual report.

Line #

```
1       On Oct. 13, I was assigned to study the salaries paid
2   to clerical employees in various titles by the city and by
3   private industry in the area.
4       In order to get the data I needed, I called Mr. Johnson at
5   the Bureau of the Budget and the payroll officers at X Corp.-
6   a brokerage house, Y Co. –an insurance company, and Z Inc. –
7   a publishing firm. None of them was available and I had to call
8   all of them again the next day.
9       When I finally got the information I needed, I drew up a
10  chart, which is attached. Note that not all of the companies I
11  contacted employed people at all the different levels used in the
12  city service.
13      The conclusions I draw from analyzing this information is
14  as follows: The city's entry-level salary is about average for
15  the region; middle-level salaries are generally higher in the
16  city government than in private industry; but salaries at the
17  highest levels in private industry are better than city em-
18  ployees' pay.
```

1. Which of the following criticisms about the style in which this report is written is MOST valid?   1.____
   - A. It is too informal.
   - B. It is too concise.
   - C. It is too choppy.
   - D. The syntax is too complex.

2. Judging from the statements made in the report, the method followed by this employee in performing his research was   2.____
   - A. *good*; he contacted a representative sample of businesses in the area
   - B. *poor*; he should have drawn more definite conclusions
   - C. *good*; he was persistent in collecting information
   - D. *poor*; he did not make a thorough study

3. One sentence in this report contains a grammatical error. This sentence *begins* on line number   3.____
   - A. 4
   - B. 7
   - C. 10
   - D. 13

4. The type of information given in this report which should be presented in footnotes or in an appendix, is the
   A. purpose of the study
   B. specifics about the businesses contacted
   C. reference to the chart
   D. conclusions drawn by the author

4.____

5. Of the following, a DISTINGUISHING characteristic of a written report intended for the head of your agency as compared to a report prepared for a lower-echilon staff member is that the report for the agency head should, *usually*, include
   A. considerably more detail, especially statistical data
   B. the essential details in an abbreviated form
   C. all available source material
   D. an annotated bibliography

5.____

6. Assume that you are asked to write a lengthy report for use by the administrator of your agency, the subject of which is "The Impact of Proposed New Data Processing Operations on Line Personnel" in your agency. You decide that the *most* appropriate type of report for you to prepare is an analytical report, including recommendations.
   The MAIN reason for your decision is that
   A. the subject of the report is extremely complex
   B. large sums of money are involved
   C. the report is being prepared for the administrator
   D. you intend to include charts and graphs

6.____

7. Assume that you are preparing a report based on a survey dealing with the attitudes of employees in Division X regarding proposed new changes in compensating employees for working overtime. Three percent of the respondents to the survey voluntarily offer an unfavorable opinion on the method of assigning overtime work, a question not specifically asked of the employees. On the basis of this information, the MOST appropriate and significant of the following comments for you to make in the report with regard to employees' attitudes on assigning overtime work is that
   A. an insignificant percentage of employees dislike the method of assigning overtime work
   B. three percent of the employees in Division X dislike the method of assigning overtime work
   C. three percent of the sample selected for the survey voiced an unfavorable opinion on the method of assigning overtime work
   D. some employees voluntarily voiced negative feelings about the method of assigning overtime work, making it impossible to determine the extent of this attitude

7.____

8. Assume that you have been asked to prepare a narrative summary of the monthly reports submitted by employees in your division.
   In preparing your summary of this month's reports, the FIRST step to take is to
   A. read through the reports, noting their general content and any unusual features
   B. decide how many typewritten pages your summary should contain
   C. make a written summary of each separate report, so that you will not have to go back to the original reports again
   D. ask each employee which points he would prefer to see emphasized in your summary

8.____

9. Assume that an administrative officer is writing a brief report to his superior outlining the advantages of matrix organization.
   Of the following, it would be INCORRECT to state that
   A. in matrix organization, a project is emphasized by designating one individual as the focal point for all matters pertaining to it
   B. utilization of manpower can be flexible in matrix organization because reservoir of specialists is maintained in the line operations
   C. the usual line-staff management is generally reversed in matrix organization
   D. in matrix organization, responsiveness to project needs is generally faster due to establishing needed communication lines and decision points

9.____

10. Written reports dealing with inspections of work and installations SHOULD be
    A. as long and detailed as practicable
    B. phrased with personal interpretations
    C. limited to the important facts of the inspection
    D. technically phrased to create an impression on superiors

10.____

11. It is important to use definite, exact words in preparing a descriptive report and to avoid, as much as possible, nouns that have vague meanings and, possibly, a different meaning for the reader than for the author.
    Which of the following sentences contains only nouns that are *definite* and *exact*?
    A. The free enterprise system should be vigorously encouraged in the United States.
    B. Arley Swopes climbed Mount Everest three times last year.
    C. Beauty is a characteristic of all the women at the party.
    D. Gil Noble asserts that he is a real democrat.

11.____

12. One way of shortening n unnecessarily long report is to reduce sentence length by eliminating the use of several words where a single one that does not alter the meaning will do.
    Which of the following sentences CANNOT be shortened without losing some of its information content?
    A. After being polished, the steel ball bearings ran at maximum speed.
    B. After the close of the war, John Taylor was made the recipient of a pension.
    C. In this day and age, you can call anyone up on the telephone.
    D. She is attractive in appearance, but she is a rather selfish person.

12.____

13. Employees are required to submit written reports of all unusual occurrences promptly.
The BEST reason for such promptness is that the
    A. report may be too long if made at one's convenience
    C. report will tend to be more accurate as to facts
    D. employee is likely to make a better report under pressure

13.____

14. In making a report, it is poor practice to erase information on the report in order to make a change because
    A. there may be a question of what was changed and why it was changed
    B. you are likely to erase through the paper and tear the report
    C. the report will no longer look neat and presentable
    D. the duplicate copies will be smudged

14.____

15. The one of the following which BEST describes a periodic report is that it
    A. provides a record of accomplishments for a given time span and a comparison with similar time spans in the past
    B. covers the progress made in a project that has been postponed
    C. integrates, summarizes, and, perhaps, interprets published data on technical or scientific material
    D. describes a decision, advocates a policy or action, and presents facts in support of the writer's position

15.____

16. The PRIMARY purpose of including pictorial illustrations in a formal report is *usually* to
    A. amplify information which has been adequately treated verbally
    B. present details that are difficult to describe verbally
    C. provide the reader with a pleasant, momentary distraction
    D. present supplementary information incidental to the main ideas developed in the report

16.____

KEY (CORRECT ANSWERS)

1.	A		6.	A
2.	D		7.	D
3.	D		8.	A
4.	B		9.	C
5.	B		10.	C

11.	B.
12.	A.
13.	C
14.	A.
15.	A.
16	B.

REPORT WRITING

EXAMINATION SECTION

TEST 1

DIRECTIONS: Each question or incomplete statement is followed by several suggested answers or completions. Select the one that BEST answers the question or completes the statement. *PRINT THE LETTER OF THE CORRECT ANSWER IN THE SPACE AT THE RIGHT.*

1. Following are six steps that should be taken in the course of report preparation:
   I. Outlining the material for presentation in the report
   II. Analyzing and interpreting the facts
   III. Analyzing the problem
   IV. Reaching conclusions
   V. Writing, revising, and rewriting the final copy
   VI. Collecting data

   According to the principles of good report writing, the CORRECT order in which these steps should be taken is:
   A. VI, III, II, I, IV, V
   B. III, VI, II, IV, I, V
   C. III, VI, II, I, IV, V
   D. VI, II, III, IV, I, V

   1._____

2. Following are three statements concerning written reports:
   I. Clarity is generally more essential in oral reports than in written reports.
   II. Short sentences composed of simple words are generally preferred to complex sentences and difficult words.
   III. Abbreviations may be used whenever they are customary and will not distract the attention of the reader.

   Which of the following choices correctly classifies the above statements in to those which are valid and those which are not valid?
   A. I and II are valid, but III is not valid
   B. I is valid, but II and III are not valid.
   C. II and III are valid, but I is not valid.
   D. III is valid, but I and II are not valid.

   2._____

3. In order to produce a report written in a style that is both understandable and effective, an investigator should apply the principles of unit, coherence, and emphasis.
   The one of the following which is the BEST example of the principle of coherence is
   A. interlinking sentences so that thoughts flow smoothly
   B. having each sentence express a single idea to facilitate comprehension
   C. arranging important points in prominent positions so they are not overlooked
   D. developing the main idea fully to insure complete consideration

   3._____

4. Assume that a supervisor is preparing a report recommending that a standard work procedure be changed.
   Of the following, the MOST important information that he should include in this report is
   A. a complete description of the present procedure
   B. the details and advantages of the recommended procedure
   C. the type and amount of retraining needed
   D. the percentage of men who favor the change

   4.____

5. When you include in your report on an inspection some information which you have obtained from other individuals, it is MOST important that
   A. this information have no bearing on the work these other people are performing
   B. you do not report as fact the opinions of other individuals
   C. you keep the source of the information confidential
   D. you do not tell the other individuals that their statements will be included in your report

   5.____

6. Before turning in a report of an investigator of an accident, you discover some additional information you did not know about when you wrote the report. Whether or not you re-write your report to include this additional information should depend MAINLY on the
   A. source of this additional information
   B. established policy covering the subject matter of the report
   C. length of the report and the time it would take you to re-write it
   D. bearing this additional information will have on the conclusions in the report

   6.____

7. The MOST desirable *first* step in the planning of a written report is to
   A. ascertain what necessary information is readily available in the files
   B. outline the methods you will employ to get the necessary information
   C. determine the objectives and uses of the report
   D. estimate the time and cost required to complete the report

   7.____

8. In writing a report, the practice of taking up the least important points and the most important points last is a
   A. *good* technique since the final points made in a report will make the greatest impression on the reader
   B. *good* technique since the material is presented in a more logical manner and will lead directly to the conclusions
   C. *poor* technique since the reader's time is wasted by having to review irrelevant information before finishing the report
   D. *poor* technique since it may cause the reader to lose interest in the report and arrive at incorrect conclusions about the report

   8.____

9. Which one of the following serves as the BEST guideline for you to follow for effective written reports?
Keep sentences
   A. short and limit sentences to one thought
   B. short and use as many thoughts as possible
   C. long and limit sentences to one thought
   D. long and use as many thoughts as possible

9.____

10. One method by which a supervisor might prepare written reports to management is to begin with the conclusions, results, or summary, and to follow this with the supporting data.
The BEST reason why management may *prefer* this form of report is that
   A. management lacks the specific training to understand the data
   B. the data completely supports the conclusions
   C. time is saved by getting to the conclusions of the report first
   D. the data contains all the information that is required for making the conclusions

10.____

11. When making written reports, it is MOST important that they be
   A. well-worded   B. accurate as to the facts
   C. brief   D. submitted immediately

11.____

12. Of the following, the MOST important reason for a supervisor to prepare good written reports is that
   A. a supervisor is rated on the quality of his reports
   B. decisions are often made on the basis of the reports
   C. such reports take less time for superiors to review
   D. such reports demonstrate efficiency of department operations

12.____

13. Of the following, the BEST test of a good report is whether it
   A. provides the information needed
   B. shows the good sense of the writer
   C. is prepared according to a proper format
   D. is grammatical and neat

13.____

14. When a supervisor writes a report, he can BEST show that he has a understanding of the subject of the report by
   A. including necessary facts and omitting nonessential details
   B. using statistical data
   C. giving his conclusions but not the data on which they are based
   D. using a technical vocabulary

14.____

15. Suppose you and another supervisor on the same level are assigned to work together on a report. You disagree strongly with one of the recommendations the other supervisor wants to include in the report but you cannot change his views.

15.____

Of the following, it would be BEST that
- A. you refuse to accept responsibility for the report
- B. you ask that someone else be assigned to this project to replace you
- C. each of you state his own ideas about this recommendation in the report
- D. you give in to the other supervisor's opinion for the sake of harmony

16. Standardized forms are often provided for submitting reports. 16.____
Of the following, the MOST important advantage of using standardized forms for reports is that
    - A. they take less time to prepare than individually written reports
    - B. the person making the report can omit information he considers unimportant
    - C. the responsibility for preparing these reports can be turned over to subordinates
    - D. necessary information is less likely to be omitted

17. A report which may BEST be classed as a *periodic* report is one which 17.____
    - A. requires the same type of information at regular intervals
    - B. contains detailed information which is to be retained in permanent records
    - C. is prepared whenever a special situation occurs
    - D. lists information in graphic form

18. In the writing of reports or letters, the ideas presented in a paragraph are usually of unequal importance and require varying degrees of emphasis. 18.____
All of the following are methods of placing extra stress on an idea EXCEPT
    - A. repeating it in a number of forms
    - B. placing it in the middle of the paragraph
    - C. placing it either at the beginning or at the end of a paragraph
    - D. underlining it

Questions 19-25.

DIRECTIONS: Questions 19 through 25 concern the subject of report writing and are based on the information and incidents described in the following paragraph. (In answering these questions, assume that the facts and incidents in the paragraph are true.)

On December 15, at 8 A.M., seven Laborers reported to Foreman Joseph Meehan in the Greenbranch Yard in Queens. Meehan instructed the men to load some 50-pound boxes of books on a truck for delivery to an agency building in Brooklyn. Meehan told the men that, because the boxes were rather heavy, two men should work together, helping each other lift and load each box. Since Michael Harper, one of the Laborers, was without a partner, Meehan helped him with the boxes for a while. When Meehan was called to the telephone in a nearby building, however, Harper decided to lift a box himself. He appeared able to lift the box, but, as he got the box halfway up, he cried out that he had a sharp pain in his back. Another Laborer, Jorge Ortiz, who was passing by, ran over to help Harper put the box down. Harper suddenly dropped the box, which fell on Ortiz' right foot. By this time, Meehan had come out of the building. He immediately helped get the box off Ortiz' foot and had both men lie down. Meehan covered the men with blankets and called an ambulance, which arrived a half hour later. At the hospital, the doctor said that the X-ray results showed that Ortiz' right foot was broken in three places.

19. What would be the BEST term to use in a report describing the injury of Jorge Ortiz?
    A. Strain   B. Fracture   C. Hernia   D. Hemorrhage

    19.____

20. Which of the following would be the MOST accurate summary for the Foreman to put in his report of the incident?
    A. Ortiz attempted to help Harper carry a box which was too heavy for one person, but Harper dropped it before Ortiz got there.
    B. Ortiz tried to help Harper carry a box but Harper got a pain in his back and accidentally dropped the box on Ortiz' foot.
    C. Harper refused to follow Meehan's orders and lifted a box too heavy for him; he deliberately dropped it when Ortiz tried to help him carry it.
    D. Harper lifted a box and felt a pain in his back; Ortiz tried to help Harper put the box down but Harper accidentally dropped it on Ortiz' foot.

    20.____

21. One of the Laborers at the scene of the accident was asked his version of the incident.
    Which information obtained from this witness would be LEAST important for including in the accident report?
    A. His opinion as to the cause of the accident
    B. How much of the accident he saw
    C. His personal opinion of the victims
    D. His name and address

    21.____

22. What should be the MAIN objective of writing a report about the incident described in the above paragraph? To
    A. describe the important elements in the accident situation
    B. recommend that such Laborers as Ortiz be advised not to interfere in another's work unless given specific instructions
    C. analyze the problems occurring when there are not enough workers to perform a certain task
    D. illustrate the hazards involved in performing routine everyday tasks

    22.____

23. Which of the following is information *missing* from the above passage but which *should* be included in a report of the incident? The
    A. name of the Laborer's immediate supervisor
    B. contents of the boxes
    C. time at which the accident occurred
    D. object or action that caused the injury to Ortiz' foot

    23.____

24. According to the description of the incident, the accident occurred because
    A. Ortiz attempted to help Harper who resisted his help
    B. Harper failed to follow instructions given him by Meehan
    C. Meehan was not supervising his men as closely as he should have
    D. Harper was not strong enough to carry the box once he lifted it

    24.____

25. Which of the following is MOST important for a foreman to avoid when writing up an official accident report?
    A. Using technical language to describe equipment involved in the accident
    B. Putting in details which might later be judged unnecessary
    C. Giving an opinion as to conditions that contributed to the accident
    D. Recommending discipline for employees who, in his opinion, caused the accident

KEY (CORRECT ANSWERS)

1.	B		11.	B
2.	C		12.	B
3.	A		13.	A
4.	B		14.	A
5.	B		15.	C
6.	D		16.	D
7.	C		17.	A
8.	D		18.	B
9.	A		19.	B
10.	C		20.	D

21.	C
22.	A
23.	C
24.	B
25.	D

TEST 2

DIRECTIONS: Each question or incomplete statement is followed by several suggested answers or completions. Select the one that BEST answers the question or completes the statement. *PRINT THE LETTER OF THE CORRECT ANSWER IN THE SPACE AT THE RIGHT.*

1. Lieutenant X is preparing a report to submit to his commanding officer in order to get approval of a plan of operation he has developed.
   The report starts off with the statement of the problem and continues with the details of the problem. It contains factual information gathered with the help of field and operational personnel. It contains a final conclusion and recommendation for action. The recommendation is supplemented by comments from other precinct staff members on how the recommendations will affect their areas of responsibility. The report also includes directives and general orders ready for the commanding officer's signature. In addition, it has two statements of objections presented by two precinct staff members.
   Which one of the following, if any, is either an item that Lieutenant X should have included in his report and which is not mentioned above, or is an item which Lieutenant X improperly did include in his report?
   A. Considerations of alternative courses of action and their consequences should have been covered in the report.
   B. The additions containing undocumented objections to the recommended course of action should not have been included as part of the report.
   C. A statement on the qualifications of Lieutenant X, which would support his expertness in the field under consideration, should have been included in the report.
   D. The directives and general orders should not have been prepared and included in the report until the commanding officer had approved the recommendations.
   E. None of the above, since Lieutenant X's report was both proper and complete.

1.____

2. During a visit to a section, the district supervisor criticizes the method being used by the assistant foreman to prepare a certain report and orders him to modify the method. This change ordered by the district supervisor is in direct conflict with the specific orders of the foreman.
   In this situation, it would be BEST for the assistant foreman to
   A. change the method and tell the foreman about the change at the first opportunity
   B. change the method and rely on the district supervisor to notify the foreman
   C. report the matter to the foreman and delay the preparation of the report
   D. ask the district supervisor to discuss the matter with the foreman but use the old method for the time being

2.____

3. A department officer should realize that the MOST usual reason for writing a report is to
    A. give orders and follow up their execution
    B. establish a permanent record
    C. raise questions
    D. supply information

4. A very important report which is being prepared by a department officer will soon be due on the desk of the district supervisor. No typing help is available at this time for the officer.
   For the officer to write out this report in longhand in such a situation would be
    A. *bad*; such a report would not make the impression a typed report would
    B. *good*; it is important to get the report in on time
    C. *bad*; the district supervisor should not be required to read longhand reports
    D. *good*; it would call attention to the difficult conditions under which this section must work

5. In a well-written report, the length of each paragraph in the report should be
    A. varied according to the content
    B. not over 300 words
    C. pretty nearly the same
    D. gradually longer as the report is developed and written

6. A clerk in the headquarters office complains to you about the way in which you are filing out a certain report.
   It would be BEST for you to
    A. tell the clerk that you are following official procedures in filling out the report
    B. ask to be referred to the clerk's superior
    C. ask the clerk exactly what is wrong with the way in which you are filling out the report
    D. tell the clerk that you are following the directions of the district supervisor

7. The use of an outline to help in writing a report is
    A. *desirable*, in order to insure good organization and coverage
    B. *necessary*, so it can be used as an introduction to the report itself
    C. *undesirable*, since it acts as a straightjacket and may result in an unbalanced report
    D. *desirable*, if you know your immediate supervisor reads reports with extreme care and attention

8. It is advisable that a department officer do his paper work and report writing as soon as he has completed an inspection MAINLY because
    A. there are usually deadlines to be met
    B. it insures a steady work-flow
    C. he may not have time for this later
    D. the facts are then freshest in his mind

9. Before you turn in a report you have written of an investigation that you have made, you discover some additional information you didn't know about before. Whether or not you re-write the report to include this additional information should depend MAINLY on the
   A. amount of time remaining before the report is due
   B. established policy of the department covering the subject matter of the report
   C. bearing this information will have on the conclusions of the report
   D. number of people who will eventually review the report

10. When a supervisory officer submits a periodic report to the district supervisor, he should realize that the CHIEF importance of such a report is that it
    A. is the principal method of checking on the efficiency of the supervisor and his subordinates
    B. is something to which frequent reference will be made
    C. eliminates the need for any personal follow-up or inspection by higher echelons
    D. permits the district supervisor to exercise his functions of direction, supervision, and control better

11. Conclusions and recommendations are usually placed at the end rather than at the beginning of a report because
    A. the person preparing the report may decide to change some of the conclusions and recommendations before he reaches the end of the report
    B. they are the most important part of the report
    C. they can be judged better by the person to whom the report is sent after he reads the facts and investigators which come earlier in the report
    D. they can be referred to quickly when needed without reading the rest of the report

12. The use of the same method of record-keeping and reporting by all agency sections is
    A. *desirable*, MAINLY because it saves time in section operations
    B. *undesirable*, MAINLY because it kills the initiative of the individual section foreman
    C. *desirable*, MAINLY because it will be easier for the administrator to evaluate and compare section operations
    D. *undesirable*, MAINLY because operations vary from section to section and uniform record-keeping and reporting is not appropriate

13. The GREATEST benefit the section officer will have from keeping complete and accurate records and reports of section operations is that
    A. he will find it easier to run his section efficiently
    B. he will need less equipment
    C. he will need less manpower
    D. the section will run smoothly when he is out

14. You have prepared a report to your superior and are ready to send it forward. But on re-reading it, you think some parts are not clearly expressed and your superior ay have difficulty getting your point.
Of the following, it would be BEST for you to
    A. give the report to one of your men to read, and if he has no trouble understanding it send it through
    B. forward the report and call your superior the next day to ask whether it was all right
    C. forward the report as is; higher echelons should be able to understand any report prepared by a section officer
    D. do the report over, re-writing the sections you are in doubt about

14.____

15. The BEST of the following statements concerning reports is that
    A. a carelessly written report may give the reader an impression of inaccuracy
    B. correct grammar and English are unimportant if the main facts are given
    C. every man should be required to submit a daily work report
    D. the longer and more wordy a report is, the better it will read

15.____

16. In writing a report, the question of whether or not to include certain material could be determined BEST by considering the
    A. amount of space the material will occupy in the report
    B. amount of time to be spent in gathering the material
    C. date of the material
    D. value of the material to the superior who will read the report

16.____

17. Suppose you are submitting a fairly long report to your superior.
The one of the following sections that should come FIRST in this report is a
    A. description of how you gathered material
    B. discussion of possible objections to your recommendations
    C. plan of how your recommendations can be put into practice
    D. statement of the problem dealt with

17.____

Questions 18-20.

DIRECTIONS: A foreman is asked to write a report on the incident described in the following passage. Answer Questions 18 through 20 based on the following information.

On March 10, Henry Moore, a laborer, was in the process of transferring some equipment from the machine shop to the third floor. He was using a dolly to perform this task and, as he was wheeling the material through the machine shop, laborer Bob Greene called to him. As Henry turned to respond to Bob, he jammed the dolly into Larry Mantell's leg, knocking Larry down in the process and causing the heavy drill that Larry was holding to fall on Larry's foot. Larry started rubbing his foot and then, infuriated, jumped up and punched Henry in the jaw. The force of the blow drove Henry's head back against the wall. Henry did not fight back; he appeared to be dazed. An ambulance was called to take Henry to the hospital, and the ambulance attendant told the foreman that it appeared likely that Henry had suffered a concussion. Larry's injuries consisted of some bruises, but he refused medical attention.

18. An adequate report of the above incident should give as minimum information 18.____
the names of the persons involved, the names of the witnesses, the date and
the time that each event took place, and the
    A. names of the ambulance attendants
    B. names of all the employees working in the machine shop
    C. location where the accident occurred
    D. nature of the previous safety training each employee had been given

19. The only one of the following which is NOT a fact is 19.____
    A. Bob called to Henry
    B. Larry suffered a concussion
    C. Larry rubbed his foot
    D. the incident took place in the machine shop

20. Which of the following would be the MOST accurate summary of the incident 20.____
for the foreman to put in his report of the accident?
    A. Larry Mantell punched Henry Moore because a drill fell on his foot and he
       was angry. Then Henry fell and suffered a concussion.
    B. Henry Moore accidentally jammed a dolly into Larry Mantell's foot,
       knocking Larry down. Larry punched Henry, pushing him into the wall
       and causing him to bang his head against the wall.
    C. Bob Greene called Henry Moore. A dolly than jammed into Larry Mantell
       and knocked him down. Larry punched Henry who tripped and suffered
       some bruises. An ambulance was called.
    D. A drill fell on Larry Mantell's foot. Larry jumped up suddenly and punched
       Henry Moore and pushed him into the wall. Henry may have suffered a
       concussion as a result of falling.

Questions 21-25.

DIRECTIONS: Questions 21 through 25 are to be answered ONLY on the basis of the
              information provided in the following passage.

A written report is a communication of information from one person to another. It is an account of some matter especially investigated, however routine that matter may be. The ultimate basis of any good written report is facts, which become known through observation and verification. Good written reports may seem to be no more than general ideas and opinions. However, in such cases, the facts leading to these opinions were gathered, verified, and reported earlier, and the opinions are dependent upon these facts. Good style, proper form, and emphasis cannot make a good written report out of unreliable information and bad judgment; but, on the other hand, solid investigation and brilliant thinking are not likely to become very useful until they are effectively communicated to others. If a person's work calls for written reports, then his work is often no better than his written reports.

21. Based on the information in the above passage, it can be concluded that opinions expressed in a report should be
    A. based on facts which are gathered and reported
    B. emphasized repeatedly when they result from a special investigation
    C. kept to a minimum
    D. separated from the body of the report

22. In the above passage, the one of the following which is mentioned as a way of establishing facts is
    A. authority
    B. communication
    C. reporting
    D. verification

23. According to the above passage, the characteristic shared by ALL written reports is that they are
    A. accounts of routine matters
    B. transmissions of information
    C. reliable and logical
    D. written in proper form

24. Which of the following conclusions can logically be drawn from the information given in the above passage?
    A. Brilliant thinking can make up for unreliable information in a report.
    B. One method of judging an individual's work is the quality of the written reports he is required to submit.
    C. Proper form and emphasis can make a good report out of unreliable information.
    D. Good written reports that seem to be no more than general ideas should be rewritten.

25. Which of the following suggested titles would be MOST appropriate for this passage?
    A. Gathering and Organizing Facts
    B. Techniques of Observation
    C. Nature and Purpose of Reports
    D. Reports and Opinions: Differences and Similarities

KEY (CORRECT ANSWERS)

1. A
2. A
3. D
4. B
5. A

6. C
7. A
8. D
9. C
10. D

11. C
12. C
13. A
14. D
15. A

16. D
17. D
18. C
19. B
20. B

21. A
22. D
23. B
24. B
25. C

TEST 3

DIRECTIONS: Each question or incomplete statement is followed by several suggested answers or completions. Select the one that BEST answers the question or completes the statement. *PRINT THE LETTER OF THE CORRECT ANSWER IN THE SPACE AT THE RIGHT.*

Questions 1-5.

DIRECTIONS: The following is an accident report similar to those used in departments for reporting accidents. Questions 1 through 5 are be answered using ONLY the information given in this report.

ACCIDENT REPORT

FROM: John Doe	DATE OF REPORT: June 23	
TITLE: Sanitation Worker		
DATE OF ACCIDENT: June 22 time 3 AM PM	CITY: Metropolitan	
PLACE: 1489 Third Avenue		
VEHICLE NO. 1	VEHICLE NO. 2	
OPERATOR: John Doe, Sanitation Worker Title	OPERATOR: Richard Roe	
VEHICLE CODE NO: 14-238	ADDRESS: 498 High Street	
LICENSE NO.: 0123456	OWNER: Henry Roe ADDRESS: 786 E.83 St.	LIC. NO.: 5N1492
DESCRIPTION OF ACCIDENT: Light green Chevrolet sedan while trying to pass drove in to rear side of sanitation truck which had stopped to collect garbage. No one was injured but there was property damage.		
NATURE OF DAMAGE TO PRIVATE VEHICLE: Right front fender crushed, bumper bent		
DAMAGE TO CITY VEHICLE: Front of left rear fender pushed in. Paint scraped.		
NAME OF WITNESS: Frank Brown	ADDRESS: 48 Kingsway	
SIGNATURE OF PERSON MAKING THIS REPORT *John Doe*	BADGE NO.: 428	

1. Of the following, the one which has been omitted from this accident report is the   1.____
    A. location of the accident
    B. drivers of the vehicles involved
    C. traffic situation at the time of the accident
    D. owners of the vehicles involved

2. The address of the driver of Vehicle No. 1 is not required because he   2.____
    A. is employed by the department
    B. is not the owner of the vehicle
    C. reported the accident
    D. was injured in the accident

3. The report indicates that the driver of Vehicle No. 2 was PROBABLY   3.____
    A. passing on the wrong side of the truck
    B. not wearing his glasses
    C. not injured in the accident
    D driving while intoxicated

2 (#3)

4. The number of people *specifically* referred to in this report is 4.____
   A. 3 B. 4 C. 5 D. 6

5. The license number of Vehicle No. 1 is 5.____
   A. 428 B. 5N1492 C. 14-238 D. 0123456

6. In a report of unlawful entry into department premises, it is LEAST important to include the 6.____
   A. estimated value of the property missing
   B. general description of the premises
   C. means used to get into the premises
   D. time and date of entry

7. In a report of an accident, it is LEAST important to include the 7.____
   A. name of the insurance company of the person injured in the accident
   B. probable cause of the accident
   C. time and place of the accident
   D. names and addresses of all witnesses of the accident

8. Of the following, the one which is NOT required in the preparation of a weekly functional expense report is the 8.____
   A. hourly distribution of the time by proper heading in accordance with the actual work performed
   B. signatures of officers not involved in the preparation of the report
   C. time records of the men who appear on the payroll of the respective locations
   D. time records of men working in other districts assigned to this location

KEY (CORRECT ANSWERS)

1.	C	5.	D
2.	A	6.	B
3.	C	7.	A
4.	B	8.	B

REPORT WRITING

EXAMINATION SECTION

TEST 1

DIRECTIONS: Each question or incomplete statement is followed by several suggested answers or completions. Select the one that BEST answers the question or completes the statement. *PRINT THE LETTER OF THE CORRECT ANSWER IN THE SPACE AT THE RIGHT.*

Questions 1-5.

DIRECTIONS: Questions 1 through 5 are to be answered SOLELY on the basis of the following report.

REPORT OF DEFECTIVE EQUIPMENT

DEPARTMENT: *Social Services*
DIVISION: *Personnel*
ROOM: 120B

REPORT NO. 3026
DATE OF REPORT: *5/27*

DEFECTIVE EQUIPMENT: *Six office telephones with pick-up and hold buttons*

DESCRIPTION OF DEFECT: *Marjorie Black, a Clerk, called on 5/22 to report that the button lights for the four lines on all six telephones in her office were not functioning and it was, therefore, impossible to know which lines were in use. On 5/26, Howard Perl, Admin. Asst., called in regard to the same telephones. He was annoyed because no repairs had been made and stated that all the employees in his unit were being inconvenienced. He requested prompt repair service.*

Ruth Gomez
SIGNATURE OF REPORTING EMPLOYEE
Sr. Telephone Operator
TITLE

JUDITH O'LAUGHLIN
SIGNATURE OF SUPERVISOR

TO BE COMPLETED AFTER SERVICING
DATE: 5/28
APPROVED: Judy O'Laughlin

---

1. The person who made a written report about the improper functioning of telephones in the Personnel division is
    A. Marjorie Black
    B. Ruth Gomez
    C. Howard Perl
    D. Judith O'Laughlin

1.____

2. How many days elapsed between the original request for telephone repair service and the completion of service?
   A. 2 B. 4 C. 5 D. 6

3. Of the following, the only information NOT given in the report is
   A. number of employees affected by the defective service
   B. number of the report
   C. number of telephones with a button defect
   D. telephone numbers of the defective phones

4. The one of the following items of information which would have been LEAST helpful to the repairman who was assigned this repair job is that
   A. the defect involved pick-up buttons for 4 serviced lines
   B. the location is Room 120B in the Department of Social Services
   C. Marjorie Black initially reported the defective equipment
   D. six telephone units need to be repaired

5. Which of the following statements is CORRECT concerning the people mentioned in the report?
   A. Ruth Gomez has a higher titled than Judith O'Laughlin
   B. Judith O'Laughlin's signature appears twice on this form
   C. Howard Perl reported on May 25 that the telephones needed adjusting
   D. Marjorie Black reported that she was disturbed that no repairs had been made

Questions 6-10.

DIRECTIONS: Questions 6 through 10 are based on the UNUSUAL OCCURRENCE REPORT given below. Five phrases in the report have been removed and are listed below the report as 1. through 5. in each of the five places where phrases of the report have been left out, the number of a question has been inserted. For each question, select the number of the missing phrase which would make the report read correctly.

UNUSUAL OCCURRENCE REPORT

POST _____
TOUR _____
DATE _____

Location of Occurrence:_____
REMARKS: While making rounds this morning, I thought that I heard some strange sounds coming from Storeroom #55. Upon investigation, I saw that 6 and that the door to the storeroom was slightly opened. At 2:45 A.M. I 7.

Suddenly two men jumped out from 8, dropped the tools which they were holding, and made a dash for the door. I ordered them to stop, but they just kept running.

3 (#1)

I was able to get a good look at both of them. One man was wearing a green jacket and had a full beard, and the other was short and had blond hair. Immediately, I called the police; and about two minutes later, I notified 9. I 10 the police arrived, and I gave them the complete details of the incident.

                                                  Security Officer Donald Rimson   23807
                                                              Signature   Pass No.

1. the special inspection control desk
2. behind some crates
3. the lock had been tampered with
4. remained at the storeroom unit
5. entered the storeroom and began to look around

6.   A. 1   B. 3   C. 4   D. 5   6.____

7.   A. 2   B. 3   C. 4   D. 5   7.____

8.   A. 1   B. 2   C. 3   D. 4   8.____

9.   A. 1   B. 2   C. 3   D. 4   9.____

10. A. 2   B. 3   C. 4   D. 5   10.____

Questions 11-13.

DIRECTIONS: Below is a report consisting of 15 numbered sentences, some of which are not consistent with the principles of good report writing. Questions 11 through 13 are to be answered SOLELY on the basis of the information contained in the report and your knowledge of investigative principles and practices.

To: Tom Smith, Administrative Investigator
From: John Jones, Supervising Investigator

1. On January 7, I received a call from Mrs. H. Harris of 684 Sunset Street, Brooklyn.
2. Mr. Harris informed me that she wanted to report an instance of fraud relating to public assistance payments being received by her neighbor, Mrs. I Wallace.
3. I advised her that such a subject would best be discussed in person.
4. I then arranged a field visitation for January 10 at Mrs. Harris' apartment, 684 Sunset Street, Brooklyn.
5. On January 10, I discussed the basis for Mrs. Harris' charge against Mrs. Wallace at the former's apartment.
6. She stated that her neighbor is receiving Aid to Dependent Children payments for seven children, but that only three of her children are still living with her.
7. In addition, Mrs. Harris also claimed that her husband, whom she reported to the authorities as missing, usually sees her several times a week.
8. After further questioning, Mrs. Harris admitted to me that she had been quite friendly with Mrs. Wallace until they recently argued about trash left in their adjoining hall corridor.

9. However, she firmly stated that her allegations against Mrs. Wallace were valid and that she feared repercussions for her actions.
10. At the completion of the interview, I assured Mrs. Harris of the confidentiality of her statements and that an attempt would be made to verify her allegations.
11. As I was leaving Mrs. Harris' apartment, I noticed a man, aged approximately 45, walking out of Mrs. Wallace's apartment.
12. I followed him until he entered an old green Oldsmobile and sped away.
13. On January 3, I returned to 684 Sunset Court, having determined that Mrs. Wallace is receiving assistance as indicated by Mrs. Harris.
14. However, upon presentation of official identification Mrs. Wallace refused to admit me to her apartment or grant an interview.
15. I am therefore referring this matter to you for further instructions.

                                                              John Jones
                                                               Supervising Investigator

11. The one of the following statements that clearly lacks vital information is Statement
    A. 8   B. 10   C. 12   D. 14

12. Which of the following sentences from the report is ambiguous?
    A. 2   B. 3   C. 7   D. 10

13. Which of the following sentences contains information contradicting other data in the above report? Sentence
    A. 3   B. 8   C. 10   D. 13

Questions 14-16.

DIRECTIONS: Questions 14 through 16 are to be answered on the basis of the following report.

To: Ralph King   Date: April 3
       Senior Menagerie Keeper   Subject:

From: William Rattner
          Menagerie Keeper

    This memorandum is to inform you of the disappearance of the boa constrictor from the Reptile Collection in the Main Building.

    This morning upon entering the room, I realized that the snake was missing. After having asked around, I am of the opinion that the boa constrictor has been stolen. Since there are no signs of forced entry, it seems likely that whoever removed the snake from the premises entered the room through a window which had been left unlocked the previous night. I, therefore, suggest that all zoo personnel be more concerned with proper security measures in the future so that something like this does not happen again.

14. Which one of the following pieces of information has been OMITTED from the report by the Menagerie Keeper?
    A. Action taken by him after his discovery that the boa constrictor was missing
    B. The date that the disappearance of the boa constrictor was noted
    C. The time that the disappearance of the boa constrictor was noted
    D. The building in which the boa constrictor was kept

    14.____

15. Based upon information contained in the above paragraph, which of the following statements would be BEST as the subject of this report?
    A. Request for more effective security measures in the oo
    B. Vandalism in the zoo
    C. Disappearance of boa constrictor
    D. Request for replacement of boa constrictor

    15.____

16. According to the above report, which of the following statements CANNOT be considered factual?
    A. The boa constrictor was being kept in the Main Building
    B. The boa constrictor is missing
    C. All zoo personnel are careless about security measures
    D. There are no signs of forced entry

    16.____

Questions 17-19.

DIRECTIONS: Questions 17 through 19 are to be answered on the basis of the Accident Report below. Read this report carefully before answering the questions. Select your answers ONLY on the basis of this report.

ACCIDENT REPORT

February 14

On February 14 at 3:45 P.M., Mr. Warren, while on the top of a stairway at the 34th Street Station, realized the *D* train was in the station loading passengers. In this haste to catch the train, he forcefully ran down the stairs, pushing aside three other people also going down the stairs. Mr. Parker, one of the three people, lost his footing and fell to the bottom of the stairs. Working on the platform, I saw Mr. Parker lose his footing as a result of Mr. Warren's actions, and I immediately went to his aid. Assistant Station Supervisor Brown was attracted to the incident after a crowd had gathered. After 15 minutes, the injured man, Mr. Parker, got up and boarded a train that was in the station and, therefore, he was not hurt seriously.

R. Sands #3214
Conductor

17. Since accident reports should only contain facts, which of the following should NOT be put into the accident report?
    A. The incident took place at the 34th Street Station.
    B. Mr. Parker was not hurt seriously.
    C. The date that the report was written
    D. Mr. Sands went to the aid of the injured an

18. The title of the person submitting the report was   18.____
    A. Porter   B. Assistant Station Supervisor
    C. Conductor   D. Passenger

19. The TOTAL number of different persons mentioned in this report is   19.____
    A. seven   B. six   C. five   D. four

Questions 20-24.

DIRECTIONS: Questions 20 through 24 are to be answered SOLELY on the basis of the following report which is similar to those used in departments for reporting accidents,

REPORT OF ACCIDENT

Date of Accident 3/21   Tim: 3:43 P.M.   Date of Report: 3/24

Department Vehicle
Operator's Name: James Doe
Title: Motor Vehicle Operator
Vehicle Code No. 22-187
License Plate No.: 3N-1234

Damage to Vehicle: Right rear fender ripped, hubcap dented, rear bumper twisted
Place of Accident: 8th Avenue & 48th Street

Vehicle No. 2
Operator's Name: Richard Roe
Operator's Address: 841 W. 68th St.
Owner' Name: Jane Roe
Owner's Address: 2792 Beal Ave.
License Plate No. 8Y-6789
Damage to Vehicle: Grill, radiator, right side of front bumper, right-front fender and headlight crushed.

Description of Accident: I was driving east on 48th Street with the green light. I was almost across 8th Avenue when Ford panel truck started forth and crashed into my rear right fender. Denver of Ford used abusive language and accused me of rolling into his truck.

Persons Injured

Name Richard Roe   Address 841 W. 68TH Street
Name _____   Address _____
Name _____   Address _____

20. Witnesses

Name Richard Roe   Address 841 W. 68th Street
Name John Brown   Address 226 South Avenue
Name Mary Green   Address 42 East Street

Report Prepared By James Doe
Title MVO Badge No. 11346

20. According to the above description of the accident, the diagram that would BEST show how and where the vehicles crashed is

20._____

A.

B.

C.

D.

21. Of the following words used in the report, the one spelled INCORRECTLY is
 A. abussive B. accused C. radiator D. twisted

21._____

22. The city vehicle involved in this accident can BEST be identified
 A. as a panel truck
 B. the Department vehicle
 C. by the Badge Number of the operator
 D. by the Vehicle Code Number

22._____

23. According to the information in the report, the right-of-way belonged to
 A. neither vehicle   B. the Department vehicle
 C. the vehicle that took it D. Vehicle No. 2

23._____

24. An entry on the report that seems to be INCORRECT is the
 A. first witness   B. second witness
 C. third witness   D. owner's name

24._____

25. Assume that the following passage is taken from a report which you, a deputy chief, receive from a battalion chief under your command. The report relates to a fire for which the department received public criticism because of delay in response and extension of fire to neighboring buildings. *Alarm from box _____ was received at 5:13 P.M. on Friday, October 2. All first alarm companies departed from quarters expeditiously but progress along the vehicle-glutted arterial thoroughfare was agonizingly slow. By dint of*

25._____

extraordinary effort and by virtue of great skill in maneuvering through impassable traffic, Engine Co. _____ arrived at the scene at 5:21 P.M. The sight which greeted them was a virtual Dante's INFERNO, of holocaust proportions. The hub of the conflagration was the penultimate structure of a row of houses, with extension impending to contiguous edifices. The MAIN fault with the above report is that it
  A. contains spelling and punctuation errors
  B. contains unnecessary details
  C. uses words not in accordance with dictionary definitions
  D. uses inappropriate language and style.

KEY (CORRECT ANSWERS)

1.	B		11.	C
2.	D		12.	C
3.	A		13.	D
4.	C		14.	C
5.	B		15.	C
6.	B		16.	C
7.	D		17.	B
8.	B		18.	C
9.	A		19.	B
10.	C		20.	A

21.	A
22.	D
23.	B
24.	A
25.	D

TEST 2

DIRECTIONS: Each question or incomplete statement is followed by several suggested answers or completions. Select the one that BEST answers the question or completes the statement. *PRINT THE LETTER OF THE CORRECT ANSWER IN THE SPACE AT THE RIGHT.*

Questions 1-4.

DIRECTIONS: Questions 1 through 4 are to be answered on the basis of the information in the report below.

On February 15, Mr. Smith and Mr. Brown were injured in an accident occurring in the shop at 10 Long Road. No one was in the area of the accident other than Mr. Smith and Mr. Brown. Both of these employees described the following circumstances.

1. Mr. Brown saw the largest tool on the wall begin to fall from where it was hanging and run up to push Mr. Smith out of the way and to prevent the tool from falling, if possible.
2. Mr. Smith was standing near the wall under some tools which were hanging on nails in the wall.
3. Mr. Brown was standing a few steps from the wall.
4. Mr. Brown stepped toward Mr. Smith, who was on the floor and away from the falling tool. He tripped and fell over a piece of equipment on the floor.
5. Mr. Brown pushed Mr. Smith, who slipped on some grease on the floor and fell to the side, out of the way of the falling tool.
6. Mr. Brown tried to avoid Mr. Smith as he fell. In so doing, he fell against some pipes which were leaning against the wall. The pipes fell on both Mr. Brown and Mr. Smith.

Mr. Smith and Mr. Brown were both badly bruised and shaken. They were sent to the General Hospital to determine if any bones were broken. The office was later notified that neither employee was seriously hurt.

Since the accident, matters relating to safety and accident prevention around the shop have occupied the staff. There have been a number of complaints about the location of tools and equipment. Several employees are reluctant to work in the shop unless conditions are improved. Please advise as to the best way to handle this situation.

1. The one of the following which it is MOST important to add to the above memorandum is
    A. a signature line
    B. a transmittal note
    C. the date of the memo
    D. the initials of the typist

2. The MOST logical order in which to list the circumstances relative to the accident is
    A. as shown (1, 2, 3, 4, 5, 6)
    B. 2, 3, 1, 5, 4, 6
    C. 1, 5, 4, 6, 3, 2
    D. 3, 2, 4, 6, 1, 5

1._____

2._____

3. The one of the following which does NOT properly belong with the rest of the memorandum is
   A. the first section of paragraph 1
   B. the list of circumstances
   C. paragraph 2
   D. paragraph 3

4. According to the information in the memorandum, the BEST description of the subject is:
   A. Effect of accident on work output of the division
   B. Description of accident involving Mr. Smith and Mr. Brown
   C. Recommendations on how to avoid future accidents
   D. Safety and accident control in the shop

Questions 5-10.

DIRECTIONS: A ferry terminal supervisor is asked to write a report on the incident described in the following passage. Questions 5 through 10 are to be answered on the basis of the incident and the supervisor's report. Your answers should be based on the assumption that everything described in the passage is true.

On July 27, a rainy, foggy day, Joseph Jones and Steven Smith were in the Whitehall Ferry Terminal at about 9:50 A.M. waiting for the 10:00 A.M. ferry to Staten Island. Smith, seated with his legs stretched out in the aisle, was reading the sports page of the DAILY NEWS. Jones was walking by, drinking ginger ale from a cup. Neither man paid any attention to the other until Jones tripped over Smith's foot, fell to the floor, and dropped his drink. Smith looked at Jones as he lay on the floor and burst out laughing. Jones, infuriated, got up and punched Smith in the jaw. The force of the blow drove Smith's head back against the bench on which he was sitting. Smith did not fight back; he appeared to be dazed. Bystanders called a terminal worker, who assisted in making Smith as comfortable as possible.

One of the other people in the terminal for the ferry was a nurse, who examined Smith and told the ferry terminal supervisor that Smith probably had a concussion. An ambulance was called to take Smith to the hospital. A policeman arrived on the scene.

Jones' injury consisted of a sprained ankle and some bruises, but he refused medical attention. Jones explained to the supervisor what had happened. Jones truly regretted what he had done and went to the local police station with the policeman.

5. Of the following facts about the above incident, which one would be MOST important to include in the ferry terminal supervisor's report?
   A. The time the next boat was due to arrive
   B. Jones was carrying a cup of ginger ale
   C. Smith was sitting with his legs stretched out in the aisle
   D. Why Smith and Jones were in the terminal

6. The MAIN purpose of writing a report of the above incident is to
   A. make recommendations for preventing fights in the terminal
   B. state the important facts of the incident
   C. blame Jones for not looking where he was going
   D. provide evidence that Smith was not at fault

3 (#2)

7. An adequate report of the above incident MUST give the names of the participants, the names of witnesses, and the
   A. date, the place, the time, and the events that took place
   B. date, the events that took place, the time, and the names of the terminal personnel on duty that day
   C. place, the names of the terminal personnel on duty that day, the weather conditions, and the events which took place
   D. names of the passengers in the terminal, the time, the place, and the events which took place

8. The supervisor asked for individuals who had witnessed the entire incident to give their account of what they had seen. Thomas White, a twelve-year-old boy said that Jones fell, got up, turned, and then hit Smith.
   Thomas White's description of the incident is
   A. *adequate*; it is truthful, straight-forward, and includes necessary details
   B. *adequate*; it shows that the incident was not started on purpose
   C. *inadequate*; he is too young to understand the implications of his testimony
   D. *inadequate*; it omits certain pertinent facts about the incident

9. Another witness, Mary Collins, told the ferry terminal supervisor that when she heard Jones fall, she looked in that direction and saw Jones get up and hit Smith, who was laughing. She immediately ran to find a terminal worker to prevent further fighting. When she returned, she found Smith slumped on the bench.
   Mrs. Collins' report is USEFUL because
   A. it proves that Smith antagonized Jones
   B. it indicates that Jones beat Smith repeatedly
   C. she witnessed that Jones hit Smith
   D. it shows that only one punch was thrown

10. Based on the description given above, which of the following would be the MOST accurate summary for the ferry terminal supervisor to put in his report?
    A. Jones fell and Smith laughed, which caused Jones to beat him until bystanders got a terminal worker to separate them.
    B. Smith was reading a newspaper when Jones fell. Then Jones hit Smith and dazed him. Smith was examined by a nurse who said that Smith had a serious concussion.
    C. Jones tripped accidentally over Smith's legs and fell. Smith laughed at Jones, who lost his temper and hit Smith, driving Smith's head against the back of a bench.
    D. Smith antagonized Jones first, by tripping him second, by laughing at him, and third by not fighting back. Smith was aided by a nurse and went to the hospital.

Questions 11-13.

DIRECTIONS: Questions 11 through 13 are to be answered SOLELY on the basis of the following report.

To: John Greene
     General Park Foreman

Date: May 5

From: Earl Jones
       Gardener

Subject:

On May 3rd, as I was finishing a job six feet from the boat-house, I observed that the hole which had been filled in last week was now not level with the ground around it. This seems to be a hazardous condition because it might cause pedestrians to fall into it. I, therefore, suggest that this job be redone as soon as possible.

11. This report should be considered poorly written MAINLY because
    A. it does not give enough information to take appropriate action
    B. too many different tenses are used
    C. it describes no actual personal injury to anyone
    D. there is no recommendation in the report to remedy the situation

11.____

12. It is noted that the subject of the report has been left out.
Which of the following statements would be BEST as the subject of this report?
    A. Observation made by Earl Jones, Gardener
    B. Deteriorating condition of park grounds
    C. Report of dangerous condition near boathouse
    D. A dangerous walk through the park

12.____

13. In order for John Greene to take appropriate action, additional information should be added to the report giving the
    A. exact date the repair was made
    B. exact location of the hole
    C. exact time the observation was made
    D. names of the crew who previously filled in the hole

13.____

Questions 14-18.

DIRECTIONS: Questions 14 through 18 consist of sets of four sentences lettered A, B, C, and D. For each question, choose the sentence which is grammatically and stylistically MOST appropriate for use in a formal written report.

14. A. It is recommended, therefore, that the impasse panel hearings are to be convened on September 30.
    B. It is therefore recommended that the impasse panel hearings be convened on September 30.
    C. Therefore, it is recommended to convene the impasse panel hearings on September 30.
    D. It is recommended that the impasse panel hearings therefore should be convened on September 30.

14.____

15.
- A. Penalties have been assessed for violating the Taylor Law by several unions.
- B. When they violated provisions of the Taylor Law, several unions were later penalized.
- C. Several unions have been penalized for violating provisions of the Taylor Law.
- D. Several unions' violating provisions of the Taylor Law resulted in them being penalized.

16.
- A. The number of disputes settled through mediation has increased significantly over the past two years.
- B. The number of disputes settled through mediation are increasing significantly over two-year periods.
- C. Over the past two years, through mediation, the number of disputes settled increased significantly.
- D. There is a significant increase over the past two years of the number of disputes settled through mediation.

17.
- A. The union members will vote to determine if the contract is to be approved.
- B. It is not yet known whether the union members will ratify the proposed contract.
- C. When the union members vote, that will determine the new contract.
- D. Whether the union members will ratify the proposed contract, it is not yet known.

18.
- A. The parties agreed to an increase in fringe benefits in return for greater worker productivity.
- B. Greater productivity was agreed to be provided in return for increased fringe benefits.
- C. Productivity and fringe benefits are interrelated; the higher the former, the more the latter grows.
- D. The contract now provides that the amount of fringe benefits will depend upon the level of output by the workers.

19. Of the following excerpts, selected from letters, the one which is considered by modern letter writing experts to be the BEST is:
- A. Attached please find the application form to be filled out by you. Return the form to this office at the above address.
- B. Forward to this office your check accompanied by the application form enclosed with this letter.
- C. If you wish to apply, please complete and return the enclosed form with your check.
- D. In reply to your letter of December _____, enclosed herewith please find the application form you requested.

20. A city employee who writes a letter requesting information from a businessman should realize that, of the following, it is MOST important to
    A. end the letter with a polite closing
    B. make the letter short enough to fit on one page
    C. use a form, such as a questionnaire, to save the businessman's time
    D. use a courteous tone that will get the desired cooperation

20.____

Questions 21-22.

DIRECTIONS: Questions 21 and 22 consist of four sentences. Choose the one sentence in each set of four that would be BEST for a formal letter or report. Consider grammar and appropriate usage.

21. A. Most all the work he completed before he become ill.
    B. He completed most of the work before becoming ill.
    C. Prior to him becoming ill, his work was mostly completed.
    D. Before he became ill most of the work he had completed.

21.____

22. A. Being that the report lacked a clearly worded recommendation, it did not matter that it contained enough information.
    B. There was enough information in the report, although it, including the recommendation, were not clearly worded.
    C. Although the report contained enough information, it did not have a clearly worded recommendation.
    D. Though the report did not have a recommendation that was clearly worded, and the information therein contained was enough.

22.____

Questions 23-25.

DIRECTIONS: In Questions 23 through 25, choose the sentence which is BEST from the point of view of English usage suitable for a business letter or report.

23. A. Answering of veterans' inquiries, together with the receipt of fees, have been handled by the Bursar's Office since the new President came.
    B. Since the new President's arrival, the handling of all veteran's inquiries has been turned over to the Bursar's Office.
    C. In addition to the receipt of fees, the Bursar's Office has been handling veterans' inquiries since the new President came.
    D. The principle change in the work of the Bursar's Office since the new President came is that it now handles veterans' inquiries as well as the receipt of fees.

23.____

24. A. The current unrest about education undoubtedly stems in part from the fact that the people fear the basic purposes of the schools are being neglected or supplanted by spurious ones.
    B. The fears of people that the basic purposes of the schools are being neglected or supplanted by spurious ones contributes to the current unrest about education.

24.____

C. Undoubtedly some responsibility for the current unrest about education must be assigned to peoples' fears that the purpose and base of the school system is being neglected or supplanted.
D. From the fears of people that the basic purposes of the schools are being neglected or supplanted by spurious ones undoubtedly stem in part the current unrest about education.

25.
A. The existence of administrative phenomena are clearly established, but their characteristics, relations and laws are obscure.
B. The obscurity of the characteristics, relations and laws of administrative phenomena do not preclude their existence.
C. Administrative phenomena clearly exists in spite of the obscurity of their characteristics, relations and laws.
D. The characteristics, relations and laws of administrative phenomena are obscure but the existence of the phenomena is clear.

25._____

KEY (CORRECT ANSWERS)

1.	C		11.	A
2.	B		12.	C
3.	D		13.	B
4.	B		14.	B
5.	C		15.	C
6.	B		16.	A
7.	A		17.	B
8.	D		18.	A
9.	C		19.	C
10.	C		20.	D

21. B
22. C
23. C
24. A
25. D

TEST 3

DIRECTIONS: Each question or incomplete statement is followed by several suggested answers or completions. Select the one that BEST answers the question or completes the statement. *PRINT THE LETTER OF THE CORRECT ANSWER IN THE SPACE AT THE RIGHT.*

1. Of the following, the BEST statement concerning the placement of *Conclusions and Recommendations* in a management report is:
   A. Recommendations should always be included in a report unless the report presents the results of an investigation.
   B. If a report presents conclusions, it must present recommendations.
   C. Every statement that is a conclusion should grow out of facts given elsewhere in the report.
   D. Conclusions and recommendations should always conclude the report because they depend on its contents.

1.____

2. Assume you are preparing a systematic analysis of our agency's pest control program and its effect on eliminating rodent infestation of premises in a specific region. To omit from your report important facts which you originally received from the person to whom you are recording is GENERALLY considered to be
   A. *desirable*; anyone who is likely to read the report can consult his files for extra information
   B. *undesirable*; the report should include major facts that are obtained as a result of your efforts
   C. *desirable*; the person you are reporting to does not pass the report on to others who lack his own familiarity with the subject
   D. *undesirable*; the report should include all of the facts that are obtained as a result of your efforts

2.____

3. Of all the non-verbal devices used in report writing, tables are used most frequently to enable a reader to compare statistical information more easily. Hence, it is important that an analyst know when to use tables.
Which one of the following statements that relate to tables is generally considered to be LEAST valid?
   A. A table from an outside source must be acknowledged by the report writer.
   B. A table should be placed far in advance of the point where it is referred to or discussed in the report.
   C. The notes applying to a table are placed at the bottom of the table, rather than at the bottom of the page on which the table is found.
   D. A table should indicate the major factors that effect the data it contains.

3.____

4. Assume that an analyst writes reports which contain more detail than might be needed to serve their purpose. Such a practice is GENERALLY considered to be
   A. *desirable*; this additional detail permits maximized machine utilization
   B. *undesirable*; if specifications of reports are defined when they are first set up, loss of flexibility will follow

4.____

2 (#3)

C. *desirable*; everything ought to be recorded so it will be there if it is ever needed
D. *undesirable*; recipients of these reports are likely to discredit them entirely

Questions 5-6.

DIRECTIONS: Questions 5 and 6 consist of sentences lettered A, B, C, and D. For each question, choose the sentence which is stylistically and grammatically MOST appropriate for a management report.

5. A. For too long, the citizen has been forced to rely for his productivity information on the whims, impressions, and uninformed opinion of public spokesmen.
    B. For too long, the citizen has been forced to base his information about productivity on the whims, impressions and uninformed opinion of public spokesmen.
    C. The citizen has been forced do base his information about productivity on the whims, impressions and uninformed opinion of public spokesmen for too long.
    D. The citizen has been forced for too long to rely for his productivity information on the whims, impressions and uninformed opinion of public spokesmen.

5.____

6. A. More competition means lower costs to the city, thereby helping to compensate for inflation.
    B. More competition, helping to compensate for inflation, means lower costs to the city.
    C. Inflation may be compensated for by more competition, which will reduce the city's costs.
    D. The costs to the city will be lessened by more competition, helping to compensate for inflation.

6.____

Questions 7-11.

DIRECTIONS: In Questions 7 through 11, choose the sentence which is BEST from the point of view of English usage suitable for a business letter or report.

7. A. It is the opinion of the Commissioners that programs which include the construction of cut-rate municipal garages in the central business district is inadvisable.
    B. Having reviewed the material submitted, the program for putting up cut-rate garages in the central business district seemed likely to cause traffic congestion.
    C. The Commissioners believe that putting up cut-rate municipal garages in the central business district is inadvisable.
    D. Making an effort to facilitate the cleaning of streets in the central business district, the building of cut-rate municipal garages presents the problem that it would encourage more motorists to come into the central city.

7.____

8. A. This letter, together with the reports, are to be sent to the principal.
    B. The reports, together with this letter, is to be sent to the principal.
    C. The reports and this letter is to be sent to the principal.
    D. This letter, together with the reports, is to be sent to the principal.

8._____

9. A. Each employee has to decide for themselves whether to take the examination.
    B. Each of the employees has to decide or himself whether to take the examination.
    C. Each of the employees has to decide for themselves whether to take the examination.
    D. Each of the employees have to decide for himself whether to take the examination.

9._____

10. A. The reason a new schedule is being prepared is that there has been a change in priorities.
    B. Because there has been a change in priorities is the reason why a new schedule is being made up.
    C. The reason why a new schedule is being made up is because there been a change in priorities.
    D. Because of a change in priorities is the reason why a new schedule is being prepared.

10._____

11. A. The changes in procedure had an unfavorable affect upon the output of the unit.
    B. The increased output of the unit was largely due to the affect of the procedural changes.
    C. The changes in procedure had the effect of increasing the output of the unit.
    D. The increased output of the unit from the procedural changes were the effect.

11._____

Questions 12-19.

DIRECTIONS: Questions 12 through 19 each consist of four sentences. Choose the one sentence in each set of four that would be BEST for a formal letter or report. Consider grammar and appropriate usage.

12. A. These statements can be depended on, for their truth has been guaranteed by reliable employees.
    B. Reliable city employees guarantee the facts with regards to the truth of these statements.
    C. Most all these statements have been supported by city employees who are reliable and can be depended upon.
    D. The city employees which have guaranteed these statements are reliable.

12._____

13. A. I believe the letter was addressed to either my associate or I.
    B. If properly addressed, the letter will reach my associate and I.
    C. My associate's name, as well as mine, was on the letter.
    D. The letter had been addressed to myself and my associate.

13._____

14. A. The secretary would have corrected the errors if she knew that the supervisor would see the report.
    B. The supervisor reprimanded the secretary, whom she believed had made careless errors.
    C. Many errors were found in the report which she typed and could not disregard.
    D. The errors in the typed report were so numerous that they could hardly be overlooked.

14.____

15. A. His consultant was as pleased as he with the success of the project.
    B. The success of the project pleased both his consultant and he.
    C. He and also his consultant was pleased with the success of the project.
    D. Both his consultant and he was pleased with the success of the project.

15.____

16. A. Since the letter did not contain the needed information, he could not use it.
    B. Being that the letter lacked the needed information, he could not use it.
    C. Since the letter lacked the needed information, it was of no use to him.
    D. This letter was useless to him because there was no needed information in it.

16.____

17. A. Scarcely had the real estate tax increase been declared than the notices were sent out.
    B. They had no sooner declared the real estate tax increases when they sent the notices to the owners.
    C. The city had hardly declared the real estate tax increase till the notices were prepared for mailing.
    D. No sooner had the real estate tax increase been declared than the notices were sent out

17.____

18. A. Though deeply effected by the setback, the advice given by the admissions office began to seem more reasonable.
    B. Although he was deeply effected by the setback, the advice given by the admissions office began to seem more reasonable.
    C. Though the setback had affected him deeply, the advise given by the admissions office began to see more reasonable.
    D. Although he was deeply affected by the setback, the advice given by the admissions office began to seem more reasonable.

18.____

19. A. Returning to the administration building after attendance at a meeting, the door was locked despite an agreement that it would be left open.
    B. When he returned to the administration building after attending a meeting, he found the door locked, despite an agreement that it would be left open.
    C. After attending a meeting, the door to the administration building was locked, despite an agreement that it would be left open.
    D. When he returned to the administration building after attendance at a meeting, he found the door locked, despite an agreement that it would be left open.

19.____

20. A. A formal business report may consist of many parts, including the following:
    1. Table of Contents
    2. List of references
    3. Preface
    4. Index
    5. List of Tables
    6. Conclusions or recommendations

    Of the following, in setting up a formal report, the PROPER order of the six parts listed is:
    A. 1, 3, 6, 5, 2, 4
    B. 4, 3, 2, 5, 6 1
    C. 3, 1, 5, 6, 2, 4
    D. 2, 5, 3, 1, 4, 6

21. Suppose you are writing a report on an interview you have just completed with a particularly hostile applicant for public assistance.
    Which of the following BEST describes what you should include in this report?
    A. What you think caused the applicant's hostile attitude during the interview
    B. Specific examples of the applicant's hostile remarks and behavior
    C. The relevant information uncovered during the interview
    D. A recommendation that the applicant's request be denied because of his hostility.

22. When including recommendations in a report to your supervisor, which of the following is MOST important for you to do?
    A. Provide several alternative courses of action for each recommendation.
    B. First present the supporting evidence, then the recommendations.
    C. First present the recommendations, then the supporting evidence.
    D. Make sure the recommendations arise logically out of the information in the report.

23. It is often necessary that the writer of a report present facts and sufficient arguments to gain acceptance of the points, conclusions, or recommendations set forth in the report.
    Of the following, the LEAST advisable step to take in organizing a report, when such argumentation is the important factor, is a(n)
    A. elaborate expression of personal belief
    B. businesslike discussion of the problem as a whole
    C. orderly arrangement of convincing data
    D. reasonable explanation of the primary issues

24. Assume that a clerk is asked to prepare a special report which he has not prepared before. He decides to make a written outline of the report before writing it in full. This decision by the clerk is
    A. *good*, mainly because it helps the writer to organize his thoughts and decide what will go into the report
    B. *good*, mainly because it clearly shows the number of topics, number of '

C. *poor*, mainly because it wastes the time of the writer since he will have to write the full report anyway.
D. *poor*, mainly because it confines the writer to those areas listed in the outline

25. Assume that a clerk in the water resources central shop is asked to prepare an important report, giving the location and condition of various fire hydrants in the city. One of the hydrants in question is broken and is spewing rusty water in the street, creating a flooded condition in the area. The clerk reports that the hydrant is broken but does not report the escaping water or the flood.
Of the following, the BEST evaluation of the clerk's decision about what to report is that it is basically
    A. *correct*; chiefly because a lengthy report would contain irrelevant information
    B. *correct*; chiefly because a more detailed description of a hydrant should be made by a fireman, not a clerk
    C. *incorrect*; chiefly because the clerk's assignment was to describe the condition of the hydrant and he should give a full explanation
    D. *incorrect*; chiefly because the clerk should include as much information as possible in his report whether or not it is relevant

25.____

KEY (CORRECT ANSWERS)

1.	C	11.	C
2.	B	12.	A
3.	B	13.	C
4.	D	14.	D
5.	B	15.	A
6.	A	16.	C
7.	C	17.	D
8.	D	18.	D
9.	B	19.	B
10.	A	20.	C

21. C
22. D
23. A
24. A
25. C

REPORT WRITING

EXAMINATION SECTION

TEST 1

DIRECTIONS: Each question or incomplete statement is followed by several suggested answers or completions. Select the one that BEST answers the question or completes the statement. *PRINT THE LETTER OF THE CORRECT ANSWER IN THE SPACE AT THE RIGHT.*

Questions 1-5.

DIRECTIONS: Questions 1 through 5 are to be answered on the basis of the Report of Offense that appears below.'

REPORT OF OFFENSE	Report No. 26743
	Date of Report 10-12
Inmate *Joseph Brown*	
Age 27	Number 61274
Sentence 90 days	Assignment KU-187
Place of offense R.P.W. 4-1	Date of offense 10/11/
Offense Assaulting inmate	
Details *During 9:00 P.M., cellblock cleanup, inmate John Jones asked for pail being used by Brown. Brown refused. Correction officer requested that Brown comply. Brown then threw pail at Jones with intent to injure him and said he would "get" Jones. Jones not hurt.*	
Force used by officer *None*	
Name of reporting officer *R. Rodriguez*	No. C-2056
Name of superior officer *P. Ferguson*	

1. The person who made out this report is 1.____
   A. Joseph Brown   B. John Jones
   C. R. Rodriguez   D. P. Ferguson

2. Disregarding the details, the specific offense reported was 2.____
   A. insulting a fellow inmate   B. assaulting a fellow inmate
   C. injuring a fellow inmate   D. disobeying a correct officer

3. The number of the inmate who committed the offense is 3.____
   A. 26743   B. 61274   C. KU-187   D. CJ-2056

4. The offense took place on 4.____
   A. October 11   B. June 12   C. December 10   D. November 13

5. The place where the offense occurred is identified in the report as 5.____
   A. Brown's cell   B. Jones' cell   C. KU-187   D. R.P.W., 4-1

Questions 6-10.

DIRECTIONS: Questions 6 through 10 are to be answered on the basis of the Report of Loss or Theft that appears below.

REPORT OF LOSS OR THEFT	Date: *12/4*	*Time: 9:15 A.M.*
Complaint made by: *Richard Aldridge*		☒ Owner
306 S. Walter St.		☐ Other – explain:
		Head of Acctg. Dept.
Type of Property: *Computer*		Value: *$450.00*
Description: *Dell Inspiron laptop*		
Location: *768 N. Margin Ave., Accounting Dept. 3rd Floor*		
Time: *Overnight 12/3 – 12/4*		
Circumstances: *Mr. Aldridge reports he arrived at work 8:45 A.M., found office door open and machine missing. Nothing else reported missing. I investigated and found signs of forced entry; door lock was broken.*		
Signature of Reporting Officer: *B.L. Ramirez*		
Notify:		
☐ Q Building & Grounds Office, 768 N. Margin Ave.		
☐ Q Lost Property Office, 110 Brand Ave. 0		
☒ Security Office, 703 N. Wide Street		

6. The person who made this complaint is
   A. a secretary
   B. a security officer
   C. Richard Aldridge
   D. B.L. Ramirez

7. The report concerns a computer that has been
   A. lost   B. damaged   C. stolen   D. sold

8. The person who took the computer PROBABLY entered the office through
   A. a door
   B. a window
   C. the roof
   D. the basement

9. When did the head of the Accounting Department FIRST notice that the computer was missing?
   A. December 4 at 9:15 A.M.
   B. December 4 at 8:45 A.M.
   C. The night of December 3
   D. The night of December 4

10. The event described in the report took place at
    A. 306 South Walter Street
    B. 768 North Margin Avenue
    C. 110 Brand Avenue
    D. 703 North Wide Street

Questions 11-15.

DIRECTIONS: Questions 11 through 15 are to be answered on the basis of the following excerpt from a recorded Annual Report of the Police Department. This material should be read first and then referred to in answering these questions, which are to be answered SOLELY on the basis of the material herein contained.

LEGAL BUREAU

One of the more important functions of this bureau is to analyze and furnish the department with pertinent information concerning Federal and State statutes and local laws which affect the department, law enforcement or crime prevention. In addition, all measures introduced in the State Legislature and the City Council, which may affect this department, are carefully reviewed by members of the Legal Bureau and, where necessary, opinions and recommendations thereon are prepared.

Another important function of this office is the prosecution of cases in the Magistrate's Courts. This is accomplished by assignment of attorneys who are members of the Legal Bureau to appear in those cases which are deemed to raise issues of importance to the department or questions of law which require technical presentation to facilitate proper determination; and also in those cases where request is made for such appearance by a magistrate, some other official of the city, or a member of the force. Attorneys are regularly assigned to prosecute all cases in the Family Court.

Proposed legislation was prepared and sponsored for introduction in the State Legislature and, at this writing, one of these proposals has already been enacted into law and five others are presently on the Governor's desk awaiting executive action. The new law prohibits the sale or possession of a hypodermic syringe or needle by an unauthorized person. The bureau's proposals awaiting executive action pertain to: an amendment to the Code of Criminal Procedure prohibiting desk officers from taking bail in gambling cases or in cases mentioned in Section 552, Code of Criminal Procedure, including confidence men and swindlers as jostlers in the Penal Law; prohibiting the sale of switch-blade knives of any size to children under 16 and bills extending the licensing period of gunsmiths.

The Legal Bureau has regularly cooperated with the Corporation Counsel and the District attorneys in respect to matters affecting this department, and has continued to advise and represent the Police Athletic League, the Police Sports Association, the Police Relief Fund, and the Police Pension Fund.

The following is a statistical report of the activities of the bureau during the current year as compared with the previous year:

	Current Year	Previous Year
Memoranda of law prepared	68	83
Legal matters forwarded to Corporation Counsel	122	144
Letters requesting legal information	756	807
Letters requesting departmental records	139	111
Matters for publication	17	26
Court appearances of members of bureau	4,678	4,621
Conferences	94	103
Lectures at Police Academy	30	33
Reports on proposed legislation	194	255
Deciphering of codes	79	27
Expert testimony	31	16
Notices to court witnesses	55	81
Briefs prepared	22	18
Court papers prepared	258	—

11. One of the functions of the Legal Bureau is to 11._____
    A. review and make recommendations on proposed federal laws affecting law enforcement
    B. prepare opinions on all measures introduced in the state legislature and the City Council
    C. furnish the Police Department with pertinent information concerning all new federal and state laws
    D. analyze all laws affecting the work of the Police Department

12. The Legal Bureau sponsored a bill that would 12._____
    A. extend the licenses of gunsmiths
    B. prohibit the sale of switch-blade knives to children of any size
    C. place confidence men and swindlers in the same category as jostlers in the Penal Law
    D. prohibit desk officers from admitting gamblers, confidence men, and swindlers to bail

13. From the report, it is NOT reasonable to infer that 13._____
    A. fewer bills affecting the Police Department were introduced in the current year
    B. the preparation of court papers was a new activity assumed in the current year
    C. the Code of Criminal Procedure authorizes desk officers to accept bail in certain cases
    D. the penalty for jostling and swindling is the same

14. According to the statistical report, the activity showing the GREATEST percentage of decrease in the current year compared with the previous year was 14._____
    A. matters for publication
    B. reports on proposed legislation
    C. notices to court witnesses
    D. memoranda of law prepared

15. According to the report, the percentage of bills prepared and sponsored by the Legal Bureau, which were passed by the State Legislature and sent to the Governor for approval, was
    A. approximately 3.2%
    B. approximately 2.6%
    C. approximately .5%
    D. not capable of determination from the data given

15.____

KEY (CORRECT ANSWERS)

1.	C	6.	C	11.	D
2.	B	7.	C	12.	C
3.	B	8.	A	13.	D
4.	A	9.	B	14.	A
5.	D	10.	B	15.	D

TEST 2

DIRECTIONS: Each question or incomplete statement is followed by several suggested answers or completions. Select the one that BEST answers the question or completes the statement. *PRINT THE LETTER OF THE CORRECT ANSWER IN THE SPACE AT THE RIGHT.*

Questions 1-2.

DIRECTIONS: Questions 1 and 2 are to be answered on the basis of the Instructions, the Bridge and Tunnel Officer's Toll Report form, and the situation given below. The questions ask how the report form should be filled in based on the Instructions and the information given in the situation.

INSTRUCTIONS

Assume that a Bridge and Tunnel Officer on duty in a toll booth must make an entry on the following report form immediately after each incident in which a vehicle driver does not pay the correct toll.

BRIDGE AND TUNNEL OFFICER'S TOLL REPORT				
Officer_____		Date_____	
	Time	Type of Vehicle	Toll Collected	Explanation of Entry
1.				
2.				

SITUATION

John McDonald is a Bridge and Tunnel Officer assigned to toll booth 4, between the hours of 11 P.M. and 1 A.M.. On this particular tour, two incidents occurred. At 11:43 P.M., a five-axle truck stopped at the toll booth and Officer McDonald collected a $2.50 toll from the driver. As the truck passed, he realized the toll should have been $3.30, and he quickly copied the vehicle's license plate number as M724HJ. At 12:35 A.M., a motorcycle went through toll lane 4 without paying the toll. The motorcycle did not have any license plate.

1. The entry which should be made on line1 in the second column is
    A. 11:43 P.M.
    B. 12:34 A.M.
    C. five-axle truck
    D. motorcycle

    1._____

2. The above passage does NOT provide the information necessary to fill in which of the following items?
    A. Officer
    B. Date
    C. Line 1, Toll Collected
    D. Line 2, Time

    2._____

2 (#2)

FACT SITUATION

Peter Miller is a Correction Officer assigned to duty in Cell-block A. His superior officer is John Doakes. Miller was on duty at 1:30 P.M. on March 21 when he heard a scream for help from Cell 12. He hurried to Cell 12 and found inmate Richard Rogers stamping out a flaming book of matches. Inmate John Jones was screaming. It seems that Jones had accidentally set fire to the entire book of matches while lighting a cigarette, and he had burned his left hand. Smoking was permitted at this hour. Miller reported the incident by phone, and Jones was escorted to the dispensary where his hand was treated at 2:00 P.M. by Dr. Albert Lorillo. Dr. Lorillo determined that Jones could return to his cellblock, but that he should be released from work for four days. The doctor scheduled a re-examination for March 22. A routine investigation of the incident was made by James Lopez. Jones confirmed to this officer that the above statement of the situation was correct,

REPORT OF INMATE INJURY	
(1) Name of Inmate	(2) Assignment
(3) Number	(4) Location
(5) Nature of Injury	(6) Date
(7) Details (how, when, where injury was incurred)	
(8) Received medical attention: date _____ time _____	
(9) Treatment	
(10) Disposition (check one or more): _____ (10-1) Return to housing area __ (10-2) Return to duty _____ (10-3) Work release _____ days ____ (10-4) Re-examine in _____ days	
(11) Employee reporting injury_____	
(12) Employee's supervisor or superior officer_____	
(13) Medical officer treating injury_____	
(14) Investigating officer_____	
(15) Head of institution_____	

3. Which of the following should be entered in Item 1?
   A. Peter Miller			B. John Doakes
   C. Richard Rogers		D. John Jones

4. Which of the following should be entered in Item 11?
   A. Peter Miller			C. James Lopez
   C. Richard Rogers		D. John Jones

5. Which of the following should be entered in Item 8?
   A. 2/21, 1:30 P.M.		B. 2/21, 2:00 P.M.
   C. 3/21, 1:30 P.M.		D. 3/21, 2:00 P.M.

6. For Item 10, which of the following should be checked?
   A. 10-4 only			B. 10-1 and 10-4
   C. 10-1, 10-3, and 10-4		D. 10-2, 10-4, and 10-4

7. Of the following items, which one CANNOT be filled in on the basis of the information given in the Fact Situation? Item
   A. 12   B. 13   C. 14   D. 15

7._____

Questions 8-11.

DIRECTIONS: Questions 8 through 11 are to be answered on the basis of the Fact Situation and the Traffic Control Report form below. Read the Fact Situation carefully, and examine the blank report form. The questions ask how the report form should be filled in based on the information given in the Fact Situation.

FACT SITUATION

Mary Fields is a Traffic Control Agent. Her City Employee Number is Z90019. She is assigned to duty at the intersection of Silver Street and Amber Avenue. On the morning of May 15, she arrives at this intersection at 9:00 A.M. and sees that there is a new *patch job* on the surface of Amber Avenue in the middle of the pedestrian crosswalk and near the northwest corner of the intersection. They day before, an emergency crew was digging here. The hole is now closed and resurfaced, but the patch job on the surface was not done very well. The patch is nearly an inch higher than the surrounding surface, and it has a sharp edge that pedestrians are likely to trip on. Mary Fields thinks this condition is dangerous, and she reports it on the Traffic Control Report form.

TRAFFIC CONTROL REPORT
DEFECTIVE EQUIPMENT OR UNSAFE CONDITION

1. Date of observation _____ 2. Time_____
2.
3. Exact location_____
4. Type of equipment or condition found to be defective or unsafe_____
5. Type of defect_____
6. Name of reporting Agent_____
7. Employee No._____ 8. Precinct No._____

---

8. Which of the following should be entered in Blank 3?
   A. Silver Street at Amber Avenue, near northwest corner
   B. Silver Street at Amber Avenue, near northwest corner
   C. Amber Avenue at Silver Street, near northeast corner
   D. Amber Avenue at Silver Street, near northwest corner

8._____

9. Which of the following should be entered in Blank 4?
   A. Pedestrian traffic signals
   B. Pedestrian crosswalk markings
   C. Surface patch
   C. Unsafe condition

9._____

10. The information called for in Blank 5 is needed to determine what kind of repairs must be made and what kind of repair crew must be sent.
    Which of the following entries for Blank 5 will be MOST useful to the people who receive this report in deciding what kind of repair crew to assign to the job?
    A. Pedestrians may stumble and fall.
    B. New patch is higher than rest of surface.
    C. Emergency crew dug a hole here.
    D. Street repairs were not done very well.

10.____

11. There is one blank on the form for which the Fact Situation does not provide the information needed.
    The blank that CANNOT be filled out on the basis of the information given is Blank
    A. 2   B. 6   C. 7   D. 8

11.____

Questions 12-15.

DIRECTIONS: Questions 12 through 15 are to be answered on the basis of the Fact Situation and the Report of Arrest form below. Questions ask how the report form should be filled in based on the information given in the Fact Situation.

FACT SITUATION

Jesse Stein is a special officer (security officer) who is assigned to a welfare center at 435 East Smythe Street, Brooklyn. He was on duty there Thursday morning, February 1. At 10:30 A.M., a client named Jo Ann Jones, 40 years old, arrived with her 10-year-old son Peter. Another client, Mary Alice Wiell, 45 years old, immediately began to insult Mrs Jones. When Mrs. Jones told her to go away, Mrs. Wiell pulled out a long knife. The special officer (security officer) intervened and requested Mrs. Wiell to drop the knife. She would not, and he had to use necessary force to disarm her. He arrested her on charges of disorderly conduct, harassment, and possession of a dangerous weapon. Mrs. Wiell lives at 118 Healy Street, Brooklyn, Apartment 4F, and she is unemployed. The reason for her aggressive behavior is not known.

REPORT OF ARREST	
(01) (Prisoner's surname)(first)(initial)	(08) (Precinct)
(02) (Address)	(09) (Date of Arrest – Month, Day)
(03) (04) (05) (Date of Birth) (Age) (Sex)	(10) (Time of arrest)
(06) (07) (Occupation) (Where employed)	(11) (Place of arrest)
(12) (Specific offenses)	
(13) (Arresting officer)	(14) (14) Officer's No.

12. What entry should be made in Blank 01? 12.____
    A. Jo Ann Jones B. Jones, Jo Ann
    C. Mary Wiell D. Wiell, Mary A.

13. Which of the following should be entered in Blank 04? 13.____
    A. 40 B. 40's C. 45 D. Middle-aged

14. Which of the following should be entered in Blank 09? 14.____
    A. Wednesday, February 1, 10:30 A.M.
    B. February 1
    C. Thursday morning, February 2
    D. Morning, February 4

15. Of the following, which would be the BEST entry to make in Blank 11? 15.____
    A. Really Street Welfare Center B. Brooklyn
    C. 435 e. Smythe St., Brooklyn D. 118 Heally St., Apt. 4F

KEY (CORRECT ANSWERS)

1.	C	6.	C	11.	D
2.	B	7.	D	12.	D
3.	D	8.	D	13.	C
4.	A	9.	C	14.	B
5.	D	10.	B	15.	C

REPORT WRITING
EXAMINATION SECTION
TEST 1

DIRECTIONS: Each question or incomplete statement is followed by several suggested answers or completions. Select the one that *BEST* answers the question or completes the statement. *PRINT THE LETTER OF THE CORRECT ANSWER IN THE SPACE AT THE RIGHT.*
Answer all questions *SOLELY* on the basis of the information contained in the report.

Questions 1-3.

DIRECTIONS: Questions 1 through 3 are based on the following report on a personnel matter concerning a member of the force. The report consists of thirty-eight numbered sentences and tabulated entries, some of which may not be correct or consistent with the principles of good police report writing.

1 Police Officer Morton, #3999, was appointed to this Department on 5/11/00. *2* A review of the officer's attendance record, since his appointment, reveals the following:

	Year	Number of Sick Calls	Total Tours Lost
3	Year	Sick Calls	Lost
4	2000	2	3
5	2001	8	14
6	2002	9	13
7	2003	0	0
8	2004	6	9
9	2005	0	0
10	2006	20	63
11	2007 (to date)	12	26

12 The officer, since his appointment date, has been the subject of disciplinary action on eleven separate occasions. *13* The attendance record indicates that Police Officer Morton has reported late for duty a total of four times since being assigned to this patrol division. *14* Listed below is a summary of Police Officer Morton's disciplinary history with the Department:

	Date	Charge	Finding	Local Trial Penalty
15	Date	Charge	Finding	Penalty
16	5/4/01	Off post	Guilty	Reprimand
17	6/6/02	Out of uniform	Guilty	1 day annual leave
18	9/4/02	Improper patrol	Guilty	5 days annual leave
19	8/20/04	Improper time sheet	Guilty	Reprimand
20	10/13/04	Lost shield	Guilty	2 days suspension
21	11/3/04	Not home on sick report	Guilty	1 day's pay
22	5/26/05	Improper blotter entries	Guilty	$25 fine
23	6/2/05	Off post	Not Guilty	----
24	4/10/06	Lost revolver	Guilty	5 days suspension
25	2/3/07	Not home on sick report	Guilty	5 days suspension
26	6/1/07	Unfit for duty	Pending	----

27 Police Officer Morton's personnel folder indicates that he has been counseled on various occasions by superior officers of the Department. *28* It would appear that said counseling has been to no avail, other than the officer's interview in December 2004 by Sergeant Green of the Deputy Chief's office. *29* As a result of that interview, the officer's sick record improved considerably for the subsequent year. *30* Police Officer Morton has been the recipient of Departmental Recognition three times, and was awarded two Excellent Police Duties and one Authority Commendation. *31* His monthly activity record indicates that the officer performs an acceptable quantity of work when compared to his peer group. *32* The officer was interviewed by the undersigned this date. *33* His record was reviewed with him and inquiry was made by the undersigned as to the existence of personal problems or other factors which might be presented in mitigation of his poor record. *34* Police Officer Morton denied any personal problems and stated that "his record was not as bad as some other officers, he has been a frequent victim of circumstances, and by and large has been singled out for harassment by all superior officers of the Department." *35* It would appear to the undersigned that the officer has still not recognized or accepted his record as being poor, nor does he accept responsibility for it. *36* It would also appear to the undersigned that both individual counseling and numerous appearances before a local trial officer have not been effective in changing the officer's attitude. *37* Furthermore, the officer's job performance has never been more than satisfactory. *38* Based upon Police Officer Morton's overall record, it is the recommendation of the undersigned that this matter (Unfit for duty, 4/12/07, charges attached hereto) become the subject of a General Trial proceeding.

1. Which one of the following sentences or tabulated entries does *NOT* contain sufficient information?

    A. 3 B. 13 C. 28 D. 31

2. Which one of the following sentences or tabulated entries does *NOT* appear in its proper sequence in the report?

    A. 2 B. 12 C. 22 D. 35

3. Which one of the following sentences or tabulated entries contains material which is *contradicted* by other information given in the report?

    A. 6 B. 21 C. 36 D. 37

KEY (CORRECT ANSWERS)

1. B
2. B
3. D

TEST 2

Questions 1-5.

DIRECTIONS: Questions 1 through 5 are based on the following report of a Firearm Discharge by a member of the force. The report consists of 28 numbered sentences, some of which may not be correct or consistent with the principles of good police report writing.

1 Investigation reveals that Police Officer K fired 4 shots from his service revolver, S&W, .38 cal., serial #C574737. *2* Responded to place of occurrence, 420 E. 105 Street, Apartment 6F, East River Houses, N.Y., N.Y., arriving at 2240 hours. *3* Also present were Captain A, Commanding Officer, 23rd Precinct; Police Officer J; and Detectives Y & Z, N.Y.C. Police Department. *4* At 2200 hours this date received notification from Headquarters Desk Supervisor, Lieutenant L, that Police Officer K, #345, assigned to and performing duty at East River Houses, had discharged his firearm. *5* Upon arrival, conferred with Lieutenant X, Commanding Officer Sub-Division C, and Sergeant N, Patrol Bureau Relief, who were already on the scene. *6* Police Officer K, when interviewed, provided the following information:

7 While performing uniformed patrol duty at East River Houses on the third platoon, he responded to 402 E. 105th Street, apartment 6F, at 2140 hours this date. *8* Response was as a result of a radio message received from Central at 2130 hours this date of an anonymous complaint of a dispute at the location. *9* The officer was performing the second tour in a set of four tours of duty on the third platoon. *10* He responded alone because Police Officer F, #291, also scheduled for duty on the third platoon at East River Houses, had called on sick report. *11* As he entered the apartment he observed Mrs. Theresa Miller, F/W/26, resident of apartment 6F, 420 E. 105 Street, (T) East River Houses, engaged in a physical struggle with one Harold Wilson (NT) M/W/22, of 658 New Jersey Avenue, Brooklyn, N.Y., and his wife, Harriet Wilson, F/W/21, same address. *12* The officer separated the combatants and restored order. *13* The female advised Police Officer K that the basis for the dispute was a failure to pay a debt owed. *14* All parties agreed not to file criminal complaints and Mr. and Mrs. Wilson started to leave the apartment. *15* At this point, Mrs. Miller withdrew a .22 calibre Rohm revolver, serial #3015, from her apron pocket and pointed it at the departing officer and the Wilsons. *16* Police Officer K, in the foyer of the apartment, turned and cautioned Mrs. Miller to drop the gun.

17 The Wilsons, observing Mrs. Miller's actions, fled the apartment. *18* Police Officer K again asked Mrs. Miller to drop the gun, whereupon she fired three shots at the officer. *19* All three shots missed, two striking the apartment door behind the officer and one, the foyer wall. *20* Police Officer K returned the fire, discharging his revolver four times.

21 All four bullets struck Mrs. Miller, two in the right arm, one in the left arm, and one in the right ankle. *22* Mr. and Mrs. Wilson, when interviewed, corroborated the police officer's version of the incident up to the point of their departure from the apartment. *23* The Wilsons then heard numerous gun shots and ran for help. *24* Both agreed that the officer's actions were most appropriate, based upon their observations of the incident.

25 Mrs. Miller was removed to Metropolitan Hospital and she was confined there in a stable condition. *26* She will be charged with attempted murder and possession of a deadly weapon. *27* Police Officer K's revolver was checked by Sergeant N and found to contain two live and four spent rounds.

28 It is the opinion of the undersigned that Police Officer K fired his revolver in accordance with the applicable laws of the State of New York and in compliance with the rules and policies of this Department.

1. Of the following, which would be the MOST logical sequence for the first five sentences of the report?

    A. 2,5,1,3,4
    B. 2, 4,1,5, 3
    C. 4,2,5,3,1
    D. 4, 2,1,3, 5

2. Which one of the following sentences contains a conclusion rather than a statement of fact?

    A. 16 B. 19 C. 22 D. 24

3. Which one of the following sentences from the report is written in such a manner as to be *ambiguous*?

    A. 8 B. 10 C. 13 D. 26

4. Which one of the following sentences from the report contains material which is CONTRADICTED by other information given in the report?

    A. 7 B. 15 C. 21 D. 28

5. Which one of the following sentences from the report contains material which is LEAST relevant to this report?

    A. 9 B. 10 C. 18 D. 25

KEY (CORRECT ANSWERS)

1. C
2. D
3. C
4. A
5. A

TEST 3

DIRECTIONS: Each question or incomplete statement is followed by several suggested answers or completions. Select the one that BEST answers the question or completes the statement. PRINT THE LETTER OF THE CORRECT ANSWER IN THE SPACE AT THE RIGHT.

1 Lieutenant John Carlson, Commanding Officer of Sub-Division Z, arrived at 300 Adam St., apt. 14 B in Charles Houses, at 1645 hours, on 12/6/ . *2* Present at that time were Mary Brown, F/B/14, who had apparently suffered lacerations of the head, Mrs. Elizabeth Brown, F/B/40, mother of Mary, and P.O. James Deere #4012 assigned to Charles Houses. *3* Mrs. Brown resides in the building, 300 Adam St., apt. 14B, with her daughter and husband, Joseph Brown, who was not present at the scene. *4* Mr. Brown was at work at the Squire Bottling Plant where he is employed as a plant shift supervisor. *5* While awaiting the arrival of the ambulance, P.O. Deere interviewed Mrs. Brown, who was obviously distraught, though uninjured. *6* Mrs. Brown stated that, at approximately 1635 hours, just after the bottle struck her daughter, she looked up and saw two male youths, who had obviously thrown the bottle, duck back from a stairhall window. *7* She further stated that she had no idea who the boys were, although she had seen them before. *8* The ambulance arrived and removed Miss Brown, accompanied by her mother, to Metropolitan Hospital. *9* Attendant George Fuentes stated that Elizabeth Brown had sustained extensive scalp lacerations, but that no other serious symptoms were manifest. *10* A complete diagnosis will be obtained from the attending physician at Morrisania Hospital. *11* A subsequent interview of Stanley Wilson, H.A. caretaker employed at Charles Houses, was conducted in the Maintenance Office at 1725 hours. *12* Mr. Wilson stated that he saw two young males run from the rear exit at 300 Adam St. just after he had heard the crash of breaking glass and the shouts from the front of the building. *13* P.O. Deere asked Mr. Wilson if he had observed anyone who might have been involved in the bottle-throwing incident.
14 Mr. Wilson furnished a description of the two possible witnesses or participants. *15* No other persons interviewed observed youths fleeing from the building.

1. Which one of the following sentences is NOT relevant to the investigation?
   A. 4 B. 5 C. 7 D. 10

2. Which one of the following sentences contains information which is *contradicted* by other information given in the report?
   A. 9 B. 11 C. 14 D. 15

3. Which one of the following sentences is NOT in proper sequence?
   A. 5 B. 6 C. 10 D. 13

4. Which one of the following sentences contains information which is *inconsistent* with other information given in the report?
   A. 3 B. 6 C. 7 D. 8

KEY (CORRECT ANSWERS)

1. A
2. A
3. D
4. D

BASIC FUNDAMENTALS OF WRITTEN COMMUNICATION

CONTENTS	Page
INSTRUCTIONAL OBJECTIVES	1
CONTENT	1
<u>Introduction</u>	1
1. <u>Business Writing</u>	1
Letters	
Selet the letter type	
Select the Right Format	
Know the Letter Elements	
Be Breef	
Use Concrete Nouns	
Use Active Verbs	
Use a Natural Tone	
Forms	4
Memoranda	5
Minutes of meetings	5
Short Reports	6
News Releases	8
2. <u>Reporting on a Topic</u>	9
Preparation for the Report	9
What is the Purpose of the Report?	
What Questions Should it Answer?	
Where Can the Relevant information be obtained?	
The Text of the Report	10
What Are the Answers to the Questions?	
Organizing the Report	
The Writer's Responsibilities	11
Conclusions and Recommendations	11
3. <u>Persuasive Writing</u>	11
General Guidelines for Writing	11
Persuasively	
Know the Source Credibility	
Avoid Overemotional Appeal	
Consider the Other Man's Point of wiew	
Interpersonal Communications	12
Conditions of Persuading	
The Persuassion campain	
4. <u>Instructional Writing</u>	13
Advances Organizers	
Practice	
Errorless Learning	
Feedback	
STUDENT LEARNING ACTIVITIES	16
TEACHERS MANAGEMENT ACTIVTIES	17
EVALUATION QUESTIONS	19

BASIC FUNDAMENTALS OF WRITTEN COMMUNICATION

INSTRUCTIONAL OBJECTIVES
1. Ability to write legibly.
2. Ability to fill out forms and applications correctly.
3. Ability to take messages and notes accurately.
4. Ability to write letters effectively.
5. Ability to write directions and instructions clearly.
6. Ability to outline written and spoken information.
7. Ability to persuade or teach others through written communication.
8. Ability to write effective overviews and summaries.
9. Ability to make smooth transitions within written communications.
10. Ability to use language forms appropriate for the reader.
11. Ability to prepare effective informational reports.

CONTENT

INTRODUCTION

Public-service employees are required to prepare written communications for a variety of purposes. Written communication is a fundamental tool, not only for the public-service occupations, but throughout the world of work. Many public-service occupations require written communication with ordinary citizens of diverse backgrounds, so the trainee should develop the ability to write in simple, nontechnical language that the ordinary citizen will understand.

This unit is designed to develop the student's ability to communicate effectively in writing for a number of different purposes and in a number of different formats. Whatever the particular purpose or format, how-- ever, effective writing will require the writer:

- to have a clear idea of his purpose and his audience;
- to organize his thoughts and information in an orderly way;
- to express himself concisely, accurately, and concretely;
- to report relevant facts;
- to explain and summarize ideas clearly; and
- to evaluate the effectiveness of his communication.

1. BUSINESS WRITING
Several forms of written communication tend to recur frequently in most public-service agencies, including:
   - letters
   - forms
   - memoranda
   - minutes of meetings
   - short reports
   - telegrams and cables
   - news releases
   - and many others

The public-service employee should be familiar with the principles of writing in these forms, and should be able to apply them in preparing effective communications.

Letters

Every letter sent from a public-service agency should be considered an ambassador of goodwill. The impression it creates may mean the difference between favorable public attitudes or unfavorable ones. It may mean the difference between creating a friend or an enemy for the agency. Every public-service employee has a responsibility to serve the public effectively and to provide services in an efficient and courteous manner. The letters an agency sends out reflect its attitudes toward the public.

The impression a letter creates depends upon both its appearance and its tone. A letter which shows erasures and pen written corrections gives an impression that the sending agency is slovenly. Similarly, a rude or impersonal letter creates the impression that the agency is insensitive or unfeeling. In preparing letters, the employee should apply principles of style and tone which will serve to create the most favorable impression.

Select the Letter Type. The two most common types of business letters are letters of inquiry and letters of response - that is, "asking" letters and "answering" letters. Whichever type of letter the employee is asked to write, the following guidelines will simplify the task and help to achieve a style and tone which will create a favorable impression on the reader.

Select the Right Format. Several styles of letter format are in common use today, including:

- the indented format,
- the block format, and
- the semi-block format.

Modified forms of these are also in use in some offices. The student should become familiar with the formats preferred for usage in his office, and be able to use whichever form the employer requests.

Know the Letter Elements. Every letter includes certain basic elements, such as:

- the letterhead, which identifies the name and address of the sender.
- the date on which the letter was transmitted.
- the inside address, with the name, street, city, and state of the addressee.
- the salutation, greeting the addressee.
- the body, containing the message.
- the complimentary close, the "good-bye" of the business letter.
- the signature, handwritten by the sender.
- the typed signature, the typewritten name and title of the sender.

In addition, several other elements are occasionally found in business letters:

- the *attention line,* directing the letter to the attention of a particular individual or his representative.
- the *subject line,* informing the reader at a glance of the subject of the letter.

- the *enclosure notation,* noting items enclosed with the letter.
- the *copy notation,* listing other persons who receive copies of the letter.
- the *postscript,* an afterthought sometimes (but not normally) added following the last typed line of the letter.

Be *Brief.* Use only the words which help to say what is needed in a clear and straightforward manner. Do not repeat information already known to the reader, or contained elsewhere in the letter. Likewise, do not repeat information contained in the letter being answered. Rather than repeat the content of a previous letter, one can say something like, "Please refer to our letter dated March 5:"

An employee can shorten his letters by using single words that serve the same function as longer phrases. Many commonly used phrases can be replaced by single words. For example,

Phrase	Single word
in order to	to
in reference to in	about
the amount of	for, of
in a number of cases	some
in view of	because
with regard to	about, in

Similarly, avoid the use of adjectives and nouns that are formed from verbs. If the root verbs are used instead, the writing will be more concise and more vivid. For example,

Noun form	Verb form
We made an adjustment on our books	We adjusted our books
We are sorry we cannot make a replacement of	We are sorry we cannot replace
Please make a correction in our order	Please correct our order

Be on the lookout for unnecessary adjectives and adverbs which tend to clutter letters without adding information or improving style. Such unnecessary words tend to distract the reader and make it more difficult for him to grasp the main points. Observe how the superfluous words, italicized in the following example, obscure the meaning: "You may be *very much* disappointed to learn that the *excessively large* demand for our *highly popular recent* publication, 'Your Income Taxes,' has led to an *unexpected* shortage of this *attractive* publication and we *sadly* expect they will not be replenished until *quite* late this year."

Summarizing, then, a *good letter is simple and clear, with short, simple words, sentences, and paragraphs. Related parts* of *sentences and paragraphs are kept together and placed in an order which makes it easy for the reader to follow the main thoughts.*

Be Natural. Whenever possible, use a human touch. Use names and personal pronouns to let the reader know the letter was written by a person, not an institution. Instead of saying, "It is the policy of this agency to contact its clients once each year to confirm their status," try this: "Our policy, Mr. Jones, is to confirm your status once each year."

Use Concrete Nouns. Avoid using abstract words and generalizations. Use names of objects, places, and persons rather than abstractions.

Use Active verbs. The passive voice gives a motionless, weak tone to most writing. Instead of "The minutes were taken by Mrs. Smith," say, "Mrs. Smith took the minutes." Instead of "The plans were prepared by the banquet committee," say, "The banquet committee prepared the plans."

Use a Natural Tone. Many people tend to become hard, cold, and unnatural the moment they write a letter. *Communicating by letter should have the same natural tone of conversation used in everyday speech.* One way to achieve a natural and personal tone in the majority of letters is through the use of personal pronouns. Instead of saying, "Referring to your letter of March 5, reporting the non-receipt of goods ordered last February 15, please be advised that the goods were shipped as requested," say, "I am sorry to hear that you failed to receive the items you ordered last February 15. We shipped them the same day we received your letter."

Forms

In most businesses and public service agencies, repetitive work is simplified by the use of *forms*. Forms exist for nearly every purpose imaginable: for ordering supplies, preparing invoices, applying for jobs, applying for insurance, paying taxes, recording inventories, and so on. While the forms encountered in different agencies may differ widely, several principles should be applied in completing any form:

- Legibility. Entries on forms should be clear and legible. Print or type wherever possible. When space provided is insufficient, attach a supplementary sheet to the form.

- Completeness. Make an entry in every space provided on the form. If a particular space does not apply to the applicant, enter there the term "N/A" (for "not applicable"). The reader of the completed form will then know that the applicant did not simply overlook that space.

- Conciseness. Forms are intended to elicit a maximum amount of information in the least possible space. When completing a form, it is usually not necessary to write complete sentences. Provide the necessary information in the least possible words.

- *Accuracy.* Be sure the information provided on the form is accurate. If the entry is a number, such as a social security number or an address, double-check the correctness of the number. Be sure of the spelling of names, No one appreciates receiving a communication in which his name is misspelled.

Memoranda

The written communications passing between offices or departments are usually transmitted in a form known as *"interoffice memorandum."* The headings most often used on such "memos" are:

- TO: identifying the addressee,
- FROM: identifying the sender or the originating office,
- SUBJECT: identifying briefly the subject of the memo,
- DATE: identifying the date the memo was prepared.

Larger agencies may also use headings such as FILE or REFERENCE NO. to aid in filing and retrieving memoranda.

In writing a memo, many of the same rules for letter-writing may be applied. Both the appearance and tone of the memo should create a pleasing impression. The format should be neat and follow the standards set by the originating office. The tone should be friendly, courteous, and considerate. The language should be clear, concise, and complete.

Memos usually dispense with salutations, complimentary closings, and signatures of the writers. In most other respects, however, the memorandum will follow the rules of good letter-writing.

Minutes of Meetings

Most formal public-service organization conduct meetings from time to time at which group decisions are made about agency policies, procedures, and work assignments. The records of such meetings are called *minutes.*

Minutes should be written as clearly and simply as possible, summarizing only the essential facts and decisions made at the meeting. While some issue may have been discussed at great length, only the final decision or resolution made of it should be recorded in the minutes. Information of this sort is usually included:

- Time and place of the call to order,
- Presiding officer and secretary,
- Voting members present (with names, if a small organization),

- Approval and corrections of previous minutes,
- Urgent business,
- Old business,
- New business,
- Time of adjournment,
- Signature of recorder.

Minutes should be written in a factual and objective style. The opinions of the recorder should not be in evidence. Every item of business coming up before a meeting should be included in the minutes, together with its disposition. For example:

- "M/S/P (Moved, seconded, passed) that Mr. Thomas Jones take responsibility for rewriting the personnel procedures manual."
- "Discussion of the summer vacation schedule was tabled until the next meeting."
- "M/S/P, a resolution that no client of the agency should be kept waiting more than 20 minutes for an interview."

Note that considerable discussion may have surrounded each of the above items in the minutes, but that only the topic and its resolution are recorded.

Short Reports

The public-service employee often is called upon to prepare a short report gathering and interpreting information on a single topic. Reports of this kind are sometimes prepared so that all the relevant information may be assembled in one place to aid the organization in making certain decisions. Such reports may be read primarily by the staff of the organization or by others closely related to the decision-making process.

Reports may be prepared at other times for distribution to the public or to other agencies and institutions. These reports may serve the purpose of informing public opinion or persuading others on matters of public policy.

Whatever the purpose of the short report, its physical appearance and style of presentation should be designed to create a favorable impression on the reader. Even if the report is distributed only within the writer's own unit, an attractive, clear, thorough report will reflect the writer's dedication to his assignment and the pride he takes in his work.

Some guidelines which will assist the trainee in preparation of effective short reports include use of the following:

- A good quality paper;
- Wide and even margins, allowing binding room;

- An accepted standard style of typing;
- A title page;
- A table of contents (for more lengthy reports only);
- A graphic numbering or outlining system, if needed for clarity;
- Graphics and photos to clarify meaning when useful;
- Footnotes, used sparingly, and only when they contribute to the report;
- A bibliography of sources, using a standard citation style.

A discussion of the organization of content for informational reports follows later in this document.

News Releases

From time to time, the public-service employees may be called upon to prepare a news release for his agency. Whenever the activities of the agency are newsworthy or of interest to the public, the agency has an obligation to report such activities to the press. The most common means for such reporting is by using the press release. Most newspapers and broadcasting stations are initially informed of agencies' activities by news releases distributed by the agencies themselves. Thus, the news release is a basic tool for communicating with the public served by the agency.

The news release is written in news style, with these basic characteristics:

- Sentences are short and simple.

- Paragraphs are short (one or two sentences) and relate to a single item of information.

- Paragraphs are arranged in *inverted order* — the most important in information appears first.

- The first or *lead* paragraph summarizes the entire story. If the reader went no further, he would have the essential information.

- Subsequent paragraphs provide further details, the most important occurring first.

- Reported information is attributed to sources; that is, the source of the news is reported in the story.

- The expression of the writer's opinions is scrupulously avoided.

- The 5 W's (who, what, why, where, when) are included.

News releases should be typed double spaced on standard 8 1/2 x 11 paper, with generous margins and at least 2" of open space above the lead paragraph. Do not write headlines - that is the editor's job. At the top of the first page of the release include the name of the agency releasing the story and the name and phone number of the person to contact if more information is needed. If the release runs more than one page, end each page with the word "-more-" to indicate that more copy follows. End the release with the symbols "###" to indicate that the copy ends at that point.

Accuracy and physical appearance are essential characteristics of the news release. Typographical errors, or errors of fact, such as misspelled names, lead editors to doubt the reliability of the story. Great care should be taken to assure the accuracy and reliability of a news release.

2. **REPORTING ON A TOPIC**

   At one time or another, most public-service employees will be asked to prepare a report on some topic. Usually the need for the report grows out of some policy decision contemplated by the agency for which full information must be considered. For example:

   - Should the agency undertake some new project or service?
   - Should working conditions be changed?
   - Are new specialists needed on the staff?
   - Or should a branch office be opened up?

   Or any of a hundred other such decisions which the agency must make from time to time.

   When called upon to prepare such a report, the employee should have a model to follow which will guide his collection of information and will help him to prepare an effective and useful report.

   As with other forms of written communication, both the physical appearance and content of the report are important to create a favorable impression and to engender confidence. The physical appearance of such reports has been discussed earlier; additional suggestions for reports are given in Unit 3. Basic guidelines follow below for organizing and preparing the content.

   Preparation for the Report

   What is the Purpose of the Report? The preparer of the report should have clearly in mind why the report is needed:

   - What is the decision being contemplated by the agency?
   - To what use will the report be put?

   Before beginning to prepare the report, the writer should discuss its purpose fully with the decision-making staff to articulate the purpose the report is intended to serve. If the employee is himself initiating the report, it would be well to discuss its purpose with colleagues to assure that its purpose is clear in his own mind.

   What Questions Should the Report Answer? Once the purpose of the report is clear, the questions the report must answer may begin to become clear. For example, if the decision faced by the agency is whether or not to offer a new service, questions may be asked such as these:

   - What persons would be served by the new service?

- What would the new service cost?
- What new staff would be needed?
- What new equipment and facilities would be needed?
- What alternative ways exist for offering the service?
- How might the new service be administered?

And so on. Unless the purpose of the report is clear, it is difficult to decide what specific questions need to be answered. Once the purpose is clear, these questions can be specified.

Where Can the Relevant Information be Obtained? Once the questions are clear in the writer's mind, he can identify the information he will need to answer them. Information may usually be obtained from two general sources:

- *Relevant documents.* Records, publications, and other reports are often useful in locating the information needed to answer particular questions. These may be in the files of the writer's own agency, in other agencies, or in libraries.

- *Personal contacts.* Persons in a position to know the needed information may be contacted in person, by phone, or by letter. Such contacts are especially important in obtaining firsthand accounts of previous experience.

The Text of the Report

What are the Answers to the Questions? Once the relevant information is in hand, the answers to the questions may be assembled.

- What does the information reveal? This activity amounts to summarizing the information obtained. It often helps to organize this summary around the specific questions asked by the report. For example, if the report asks in one part, "What are the costs of the new service likely to be?" one section of the report should summarize the information gathered to answer this question.

Organizing the Report. The organization of a report into main and subsections depends upon the nature of the report. Reports will differ widely in their organization and treatment. In general, however, the report should generally follow the pattern previously discussed. That is, reports which generally include the following subjects in order will be found to be clear in their intent and to communicate effectively:

- *Description of problem or purpose.* Example: "One problem facing our agency is whether or not we should extend our hours of operation to better serve the public. This report is intended to examine the problem and make recommendations."

- *Questions to be answered.* Example: "In examining this problem, answers were sought to the following questions: What persons would be served? What would it cost? What staff would be needed?"

- *Information sources.* Example: "To answer these questions, letters of complaint for the past three years were examined. Interviews with clients were conducted by phone and in person, phone interviews were conducted with the agency directors in Memphis, Philadelphia, and Chicago,"

- *Summary of findings.* Example: "At least 25 percent of the agency's clients would be served better by evening or Saturday service. The costs of operating eight hours of extended service would be negligible, since the service could be provided by rescheduling work assignments. The present staff report they would be inconvenienced by evening and Saturday work assignments."

<u>The Writer's Responsibilities.</u> It is the writer's responsibility to address finally the original purpose of the report. Once the questions have been answered, an informed judgment can be made as to the decision facing the agency. It is at this stage that the writer attempts to draw conclusions from the information he has gathered and summarized. For example, if the original purpose of the report was to help make a decision about whether or not the agency should offer a new service, the writer should draw conclusions from the information and recommend either for or against the new service.

<u>Conclusions and Recommendations.</u> Example: "It appears that operating during extended hours would better serve a significant number of clients. The writer recommends that the agency offer this new service. The present staff should be given temporary assignments to cover the extended hours. As new staff are hired to replace separating persons, they should be hired specifically to cover the extended hours."

3. <u>PERSUASIVE WRITING</u>

Often in life, people are called upon to persuade individuals and groups to adopt ideas believed to be good, or attitudes favorable to ideas thought to be worthwhile or behavior believed to be beneficial. The public service employee may find he must persuade the staff of his own agency, his superiors, the clients of the agency, or the general public in his community.

Persuading others by means of written and other forms of communication is a difficult task and requires much practice. Some principles have emerged from the study of persuasion which may provide some guidelines for developing a model for persuasive writing.

General Guidelines for Writing Persuasively

Know the Credibility of the Source. People are more likely to be persuaded by a message they perceive originates from a trustworthy source. Their trust is enhanced if the source is seen as authoritative, or knowledgeable on the issue discussed in the message. Their trust is increased also if the source appears to have nothing to gain either way, has no vested interest in the final decision. Then, the assertions made in persuasive writing should be backed up by referencing trustworthy and disinterested information sources.

Avoid Overemotional Appeals. Appealing to the common emotions of man—love, hate, tear, sex, etc.—can have a favorable effect on the outcome of a persuasive message. But care should be taken because, if the appeal is too strong, it can lead to a reverse effect. For example, if an agency wanted to persuade the public to get chest X-rays, it would have much greater chance of success if it adopted a positive and helpful attitude rather than trying to frighten them into this action. For instance, appealing mildly to the sense of well-being which accompanies knowledge of one's own good health, instead of shocking the public by showing horror pictures of patients who died from lack of timely X-rays.

Consider the Other Man's Point of View. To persuade another to one's own point of view, should the writer include information and arguments contrary to his own position? Or should he argue only for his own side?

Generally, it depends on where most of the audience stand in the first place. If most of the audience already favor the position being advocated, then the writer will probably do better including only information favorable to his position. However, if the greater part of the audience are likely to oppose this position, then the writer would probably be better off including their arguments also. In this case, he may be helping his cause by rebutting the opposing arguments as he introduces them into the writing.

An example of this technique might occur in arguing for such an idea as a four-day, forty-hour workweek. Thus: "Many people feel that the ten-hour day is too long and that they would arrive home too late for their regular dinner hour. But think! If you have dinner a littler later each night, you'll have a three-day weekend every week. More days free to go fishing, or camping. More days with your wife and children." That is good persuasive writing!

Interpersonal Communications

The important role of interpersonal communication in persuading others—face-to-face and person-to-person communications—has been well documented. Mass mailings or printed messages will likely have less effect than personal letters and conversations between persons already known to each other. In any persuasion campaign the personal touch is very important.

An individual in persuading a large number of persons will likely be more effective if he can organize a letter-writing campaign of persuasive messages written by persons favorable to his position to their friends and acquaintances, than if his campaign is based upon sending out a mass mailing of a printed message.

Conditions for Persuading. In order for an audience of one or many to be persuaded in the manner desired, these conditions must be met:

- the audience must be *exposed* to the message,
- members of the audience must *perceive* the intent of the message,
- they must *remember* the message afterwards,
- each member must *decide* whether or not to adopt the ideas.

Each member of the audience will respond to a message differently. While every person may receive the message, not everyone will read it. Even among those who read it, not everyone will perceive it in the same way. Some will remember it longer than others. Not everyone will decide to adopt the ideas. These effects are called *selective exposure, selective perception, selective retention,* and *selective decision.*

The Persuasion Campaign. How can one counteract these selective effects in persuading others? One thing that is known is that *people tend to be influenced by persuasive messages which they are already predisposed to accept.* This means a person is more likely to persuade people a little than to persuade them a lot.

In planning a persuasion campaign, therefore, the messages should be tailored to the audiences. Success will be more likely if one starts with people who believe *almost* as the writer wants to persuade them to believe—people who are most likely to agree with the position advocated.

The writer also wants to use arguments based on values the particular audience already accepts. For example, in advocating a new teen-age job program, he might argue with business men that the program will help business; with parents, that it will build character; with teachers, that it is educational; with taxpayers, that it will reduce future taxes; and so on.

The idea is to find some way to make sure that each member of the particular audiences reached can see an advantage for himself, and for the writer to then tailor the messages for those audiences.

4. INSTRUCTIONAL WRITING

Another task that the public-service employee may expect to face from time to time is the instruction of some other person in the performance of a task. This may sometimes involve preparing written instructions to other employees in the unit, or preparing a training manual for new employees.

It may sometimes involve preparing instructional manuals for clients of the unit, such as "How to Apply for a Real Estate License," "How to Bathe your Baby," or "How to Recognize the Symptoms of Heart Disease."

Whatever the purpose or the audience, certain principles of instruction may be applied which will help make more effective these instructional or training communications. These are: *advance organizers, practice, errorless learning,* and *feedback.*

Advance Organizers

At or near the beginning of an instructional communication, it helps the learner if he is provided with what can be called an "advance organizer." This element of the communication performs two functions:

- it provides a framework or "map" for the leader to organize the information he will encounter,
- it helps the learner perceive his purpose in learning the tasks which will follow.

The first paragraphs in this section, for example, serve together as an advance organizer. The trainee is informed that he may be called upon to perform these tasks in his job *(perceived purpose),* and that he will be instructed in advance organizers, practice, errorless learning, and feedback *(framework, or "map").*

Practice

The notion of *practice makes perfect* is a sound instructional principle. When trying to teach someone to perform a task by means of written communication, the writer should build in many opportunities for practicing the task, or parts of it. This built-in practice should be both appropriate and active:

- *Appropriate practice* is practice which is directly related to learning the tasks at hand.

- *Active practice* is practice in actually performing the task at hand or parts of it, rather than simply reading about the task, or thinking about it.

By inserting questions into the text of the communication, by giving practice quizzes, exercises, or field work, one can build into his instructional communication the kind of practice necessary for the reader to readily learn the task.

Errorless Learning

The practice given learners should be easy to do. That is, they should not be asked to practice a task if they are likely to make a lot of mistakes. When a mistake is practiced it is likely to recur again and again, like spelling "demons," which have been spelled wrong so often it's difficult to recall the way they should be spelled. Because it is better to practice a task right from the first, it is important that learners do not make errors in practice.

- One method for encouraging correct practice is to give the reader hints, or *prompts,* to help him practice correctly.

- Another method is to instruct him in a logical sequence a little bit at a time. Don't try to teach everything at once. Break the task down into small parts and teach each part of the task in order. Then give the learner practice in each part of the task before giving him practice in the whole thing.

- A third way of encouraging errorless learning is to build in practice and review throughout the communication. The learner may forget part of the task if the teacher doesn't review it with him from time to time.

Remember, people primarily learn from what they do, so build in to the instructional communication many opportunities for the learner to practice correctly all of the parts of the task required for learning, first separately and then all together.

Feedback

The reader, or learner, can't judge how well he is learning the task unless he is informed of it. In a classroom situation, the teacher usually confirms that the learner has been successful, or points out the errors he made, and provides additional instruction. An instructional communication can also help learners in the same way, by providing *feedback* to the learner.

Following practice, the writer should include in his instructional communication information which will let the reader know whether he performed the task correctly. In case he didn't, the writer should also include some further information which will help the reader perform it correctly next time. This feedback, then, performs two functions:

- it helps the learner confirm that his practice was done correctly, and

- it helps him correct his performance of the task in case he made any errors.

Feedback will be most helpful to the learner if it occurs immediately following practice. The learner should be brought to know of his success or his errors just as soon as possible after practice.

STUDENT LEARNING ACTIVITIES

- Write "asking" and "answering" letters, and answer a letter of complaint, using the format assigned by the teacher.

- Write memoranda to other "offices" in a fictitious organization. Plan a field trip using only memos to communicate with other students in the class.

- Take minutes of a small group meeting. Or attend a meeting of the school board and take minutes.

- Write a short report on a public service occupation of special interest to you.

- Write a 15-word telegram reserving a single room at a hotel and asking to be picked up at the airport.

- Write a news release announcing a new service offered to the public by your agency.

- Based upon hearing a reading or pretaping of a report, summarize the report in news style.

- View films on effective communication, for example, *Getting the Facts, Words that Don't Inform,* and *A Message to No One.*

- For a given problem or purpose, compile a list of specific questions you would need to answer to write a report on the topic.

- For a given list of questions, discuss and compile a list of information sources relevant to the questions.

- As a member of a group, consider the problem of "What field trip should the class take to help students learn how to write an effective news release?" What questions will you need to answer? Where will you obtain your information?

- As a member of a group, gather the information and prepare a short report based on it for presentation to the class.

- Write a report on a problem assigned by your teacher.

- Write a brief persuasive letter to a friend on a given topic. Assume he does not already agree with you. Apply principles of source credibility, emotional appeals, and one or both sides of the issue to persuade him.

- Plan a persuasive campaign to persuade a given segment of your community to take some given action.

- Write a short instructional communication on a verbal learning task assigned by your teacher.

- Write a short instructional communication on a learning task which involves the operation of equipment.

- Try your instructional communications with a fellow student to check for errors during practice.

TEACHER
MANAGEMENT
ACTIVITIES

- Have students practice letter writing. Assign letters of "asking" and "answering." Read them a letter of complaint and ask them to write an answering letter. Establish common rules of format and style for each assignment. Change the rules from time to time to give practice in several styles.

- Have small groups plan an event, such as a field trip, assigning the various tasks to one another using only memoranda. Evaluate the effectiveness of each group's memo writing by the speed and completeness of their planning.

- Have the class attend a public meeting. Assign each the task of taking the minutes. Evaluate the minutes for brevity and completeness.

- Encourage each student to prepare a short report on a public service occupation of special interest to himself.

- Give the students practice in writing 15-word telegrams.

- Have the students prepare a news release announcing some new service offered to the public, such as "Taxpayers can now obtain help from the Internal Revenue Service in completing their income tax forms as a result of a new service now being offered by the agency."

- Give the students practice in summarizing and writing leads by giving them the facts of a news event and asking them to write a one or two-sentence lead summarizing the significant facts of the event.

- Read a speech or a story. Have students write a summary and a report of the speech or story in news style.

- Show films on effective communication, for example, *Getting the Facts, Words that Don't Inform,* and *A Message to No One.*

- State a general problem and have each student prepare a list of the specific questions implied by the problem.

- State a list of specific questions and discuss with the class the sources of information which might bear upon each of the questions.

- Have small groups consider and write short reports jointly on the general problem, "What field trip should the class take to help students learn how to write an effective news release?" Have each group identify the specific questions to be answered, with sources for needed information.

- Have each student identify and prepare a short report on a general problem of interest.

- Assign students to work in groups of three or four to draft a letter to a friend to persuade him to make a contribution to establish a new city art museum.

- Assign the students to groups of five or six, each group to map out a persuasive campaign on a given topic. Some topics are "Give Blood," "Get Chest X-Ray," "Quit Smoking," "Don't Litter," "Inspect Your House Wiring," etc.

- Have each student identify a simple verbal learning task and prepare an instructional communication to teach that task to another student not familiar with the task.

- Have each student prepare an instructional manual designed to train someone to operate some simple piece of equipment, such as an adding machine, a slide projector, a tape recorder, or something of similar complexity.

- Have each student try his instructional communication out on another student, unfamiliar with the task. He should observe the activities and responses of the trial student to identify errors made in practice. He should revise the communication, adding practice, review, and prompts wherever needed to reduce errors in practice.

EVALUATION QUESTIONS

Written Communications

1. Which type of letter would be correct for a public service worker to send?

    A. A letter containing erasures
    B. A letter reflecting goodwill
    C. A rude letter
    D. An impersonal letter

2. Memos usually leave out:

    A. Complimentary closings
    B. The name of the sender
    C. The name of the addressee
    D. The date the memo was sent

3. A good business letter would not contain:

    A. Short, simple words, sentences, and paragraphs
    B. Information contained in the letter being answered
    C. Concrete nouns and active verbs
    D. Orderly placed paragraphs

4. In writing business letters it is important to:

    A. Use a conversational tone
    B. Use a hard, cold tone
    C. Use abstract words
    D. Use a passive tone

5. Messages between departments in an agency are usually sent by:

    A. Letter
    B. Memo
    C. Telegram
    D. Long reports

6. Repetitive work can be simplified by the use of:

    A. Memos
    B. Telegrams
    C. Forms
    D. Reports

7. In filling out forms and applications, it is important to be:

    A. Legible
    B. Complete
    C. Accurate
    D. All of the above

8. Memos should be:

   A. Clear
   B. Brief
   C. Complete
   D. All of the above

9. Minutes of meetings should not include:

   A. The opinions of the recorder
   B. The approval of previous minutes
   C. The corrections of previous minutes
   D. The voting members present

10. Reports are written by public service workers to:

    A. Assemble information in one place
    B. Aid the organization in making decisions
    C. Inform the public and other agencies
    D. All of the above

11. News releases should include:

    A. A lead paragraph summarizing the story
    B. Long paragraphs about many topics
    C. The writer's opinion
    D. All of the above

12. Readers of news releases and reports are influenced by the:

    A. Content of the material
    B. Accuracy of the material
    C. Physical appearance of the material
    D. All of the above

13. The contents of a report should include:

    A. A description of the problem
    B. The questions to be answered
    C. Unimportant information
    D. A summary of findings

14. People tend to be influenced easier if:

    A. They can see something in the position that would be advantageous to them
    B. They are almost ready to agree anyhow
    C. The appeal to the emotions is not overly strong
    D. All of the above

KEY (CORRECT ANSWERS)

1. B
2. A
3. B
4. A
5. B

6. C
7. D
8. D
9. A
10. D

11. A
12. D
13. C
14. D

REPORT WRITING

TABLE OF CONTENTS

1. General	1
2. Purpose of Written Reports	1
3. Kinds of Reports	3
4. The Staff Study Report	3
5. Completed Staff Work	6
6. The Technical Report	6

REPORT WRITING

1. General

A government worker is frequently required to investigate a situation and to submit a report. Not all headquarters or individuals in the field want the same type of report. A report satisfactory for one purpose may be inadequate for another. When you prepare a report, you should adhere to a pattern of organization. Regard the suggestions and examples given here as guides, not law. If you decide to follow any one of the examples, do so because it most nearly meets your needs. Feel free to alter the pattern.

Many kinds of reports are written. They are not always easily distinguished from other types of communications. A simple statement of the progress one has made on his job may be prepared on a preprinted form. Other informal reports may be prepared in the form of letters or memorandums. Some reports are more formal and include drawings, charts, tables, exhibits, footnotes and bibliographies.

2. Purpose of Written Reports

Why write reports? Reports are written because they:
- Help to accurately transmit information
- Serve as records for later reference
- Provide an economical means of keeping other agencies informed

Reports are regularly read by people beyond the man to whom they are addressed. So you should ask yourself: Have I written this report as though it would stop with the man to whom it is submitted? Or have I taken into account the possibility that others may read it?

If the report goes beyond the originating office, you cannot assume that the background information will be known. Even if it is known, your report should recall and restate it. If the report goes outside your organization, it must be complete.

If you are not sure that the report will remain within the office, prepare it with the completeness and clarity necessary for readers with varying backgrounds. Furthermore, organize it so that each reader need only go so far into the report as his interest or position demands. The most effective report tells the reader at the start what is taken up and in what order.

Any report you write involves at least two persons – you and the one receiving it. You will certainly know what you want to get across, but your report will succeed only if the reader understands it.

Since the primary purpose of a report is to inform, it seems reasonable to judge it from the reader's point of view. You should ask yourself: What can I tell him?

The reader will want to know the situation immediately. When the report is short, this point takes care of itself; but when the report is long, the reader wants to be spared the problem of considering a long list of facts before learning what to do with them. What he needs is some preparation so that he will know what is coming later and what the connection is.

Next, the reader wants to know the extent of his interest in the report. Reports are generally passed along to a number of readers. Each may have a different interest. The man who receives a report usually asks: What do I need from this report? How much of it must I read? He doesn't want to bother with facts or problems that do not concern him.

The reader wants the report to show clearly what is expected of him. He does not like to be left up in the air. A report, then, should answer the following questions:
- What is the subject?
- Why should I be interested?
- What is the story in a nutshell?
- What action is recommended? Why?
    and frequently -
- Who else is interested?

Detailed development of the answers to these five questions provides the material for your report.

What Is The Subject?

The first step is to identify the subject so that the reader will know at once the subject matter of the report. Then include enough detail to show the nature of the problem. This can usually be accomplished in the opening sentence. Don't include minor details that have no bearing on the subject.

Why Should I be Interested?

Or the question may be: What difference does that make to me? The answer to this question brings the reader into the report by showing how it affects him. If the report is going to the right man, the relationship between the subject matter of the report and his interests can be quickly shown.

What Is The Story In A Nutshell?

All the pertinent facts should be stated. Do not shorten the report to the extent of omitting necessary information. Consider the previous knowledge the reader has on the subject. Remember that he must have all the background facts or history to understand the problem. Arrange these facts in a related flow. A haphazard listing of facts may be misleading.

What Action Is Recommended?

The real purpose of most reports is to get the reader to do something about the matter discussed in the report. Given the facts, the reader now wants to know if he is expected to make a decision, approve the action already taken, or simply note the information. He will also want to know the reasoning used in arriving at the conclusion. It may be helpful to list the advantages of the proposed solution and show how these advantages outweigh the disadvantages.

Who Else Is Interested?

Frequently the action you recommend will affect other activities. Be certain that your report shows the relationship between these activities and your recommendation. If the material is so voluminous that it makes your report unwieldy and breaks its continuity, place as much as possible of this material in attachments.

3. Kinds of Reports
Often the type of report is clearly indicated; for example, an accident report or a work-study report. More often you must decide for yourself the type of report needed. You can usually get some suggestions by considering how it may be used. There is, however, no magic formula for designing reports. On the contrary, there are possibly as many different types of reports as there are situations calling for reports.

Reports have been classified in many ways. The following classifications are not all-inclusive but may be of help:

Informal and Formal Reports
An elementary classification is that of informal or formal report. The informal report is usually a letter. It customarily carries four items besides the text proper: office symbol or name of person responsible for the letter, date submitted, subject, and office or person to whom submitted.

The formal report often requires the full-dress treatment, including cover, title page, letter of transmittal, summary sheet, text, attachments, and perhaps an index and bibliography.

Reports Classified According To Purpose
Reports may also be classified according to their purpose. In many instances the following reports may overlap in the way they are written:

In the problem-determining report you attempt to find the causes underlying the problem or to find out whether or not a problem really exists.

In the fact-finding report you gather and present data in a logical order, without an attempt to draw conclusions.

In the performance report you present information on the status of activities or operations.

In the technical report you present data on a specialized subject.

In the problem-solution report or staff study report you analyze the thought process that lies behind the solution of a particular problem. Since the elements of each of the above-mentioned reports may be found in the staff study report and the technical report, we will limit our discussion to these two types of reports.

4. The Staff Study Report
The staff study report is a problem-solution type of report. It presents data collected, discusses possible solutions to the problem, and indicates the best solution. It is not a form for solving a problem. You should mentally solve your problem, then report the solution in writing.

When you are ready to write, you may find the format of the staff study report useful. The format usually has a heading, a body, an ending, and when necessary, attachments.

Heading Of The Staff Study Report
The heading contains the following information:

After the "Reply to Attn of" caption, type in the office symbol or abbreviated title of the agency or headquarters originating the study. If appropriate, add the name of the individual who prepared the study. After the caption "Subject," give the subject of your study, being as brief and concise as possible. However, use a few extra words if this makes your subject more meaningful to the reader. The "To" caption should be left blank. This will allow the study to seek its own level.

Body Of The Staff Study Report

The body of the report contains five elements, or sections: (1) "Problem," (2) "Factors Bearing on the Problem," (3) "Discussion," (4) "Conclusion," and (5) "Action Recommended." These parts can be identified with the steps of problem solving:

Steps of Problem Solving	Body of Staff Study
1. Recognize the problem	1. Problem
2. Gather data	2. Factors bearing on the problem
3. List possible solutions	3. Discussion
4. Test possible solutions	4. Conclusion (a brief restatement of final solution)
5. Select final solution	
6. Act	5. Action recommended

That is why the staff study report is a convenient form for reporting your solution to a problem.

Problem: The statement of the problem tells the reader what you are trying to solve. It is ineffective to state a problem as a fact, thus: Personnel of this agency (or bureau) fail to observe discipline. It is better to state the problem in one of the following ways:

As a question: What should we do to enforce discipline in this agency?
As an infinitive phrase: To find ways to enforce discipline in this agency.
As a statement of need or purpose: This agency (or bureau) needs to develop procedures for enforcing discipline.

No discussion is necessary at this point; a simple statement of the problem is sufficient. You will have sufficient opportunity to discuss all aspects of the problem later on in the report.

Factors Bearing on the Problem: This section contains the facts, assumptions, criteria, and definitions which you used to build possible solutions to your problem. A fact is a statement of truth which can be proved. An assumption is a statement which may or may not be true, but, for the purpose of the problem, must be accepted as the basis for your reasoning. Criteria are those standards, requirements, or limitations used to test possible solutions. Devote separate paragraphs to facts, assumptions, criteria, and definitions.

Obviously, if you write a report in which you have no assumptions or definitions, it is permissible to omit either or both. Include only those important factors which you used to solve your problem. Whatever is included should be stated briefly. When material to support factors is lengthy, use attachments. Make each sentence complete enough so that the reader is not forced to refer to the attachments to understand what he is reading. A sequence of thought should be maintained throughout the body of the staff study.

Discussion: This section shows the logic used in solving the problem. It may be handled in various ways depending upon the problem being reported. Some type of introduction is desirable. Generally, some background information is necessary to properly introduce your problem. The introduction may be only one paragraph; but it could contain several paragraphs, depending on the detail required.

Most problems solved by a management intern will fall into one of the three patterns listed below. But do not try to force your report into one of these patterns if it does not appear to fit.

Pattern I: *Single best possible solution*

This is the basic and most commonly used pattern. A single best solution is selected from several possible solutions. Following is one outline for reporting on this type of problem:
 1. List all possible solutions that you think your superior would be interested in.
 2. Show how you tested each possible solution against the criteria, listing both the advantages and disadvantages. Use the same criteria for each possible solution.
 3. Show how you weighed each possible solution against the others in selecting the best possible solution.
 4. Clearly indicate the best possible solution.

Pattern II: *Combination of possible solutions*

You may need to combine two or more possible solutions for your best possible solution. Following is one possible outline for reporting on this type of problem:
 1. List all the possible solutions that you think your superior will be interested in.
 2. Show how you tested each possible solution against the criteria, listing both advantages and disadvantages. Use the same criteria for each possible solution.
 3. Show how you weighed each possible solution against the other possible solutions and why each one was retained as a partial solution to the problem.
 4. Show how and why the retained possible solutions are combined to solve your problem.

Pattern III: *Single possible solution*

At times you may want to report on only one possible solution to a problem. The following outline can be used in reporting the problem:
 1. List your single solution.
 2. Test it against the criteria.
 3. Show how and why this solution will solve the problem.

No matter how your report is organized, these points are important: (1) make it brief; (2) maintain a sequence of thought throughout; (3) show the reader how you reasoned the problem through; and (4) use attachments for support, but include enough information in the body of the report to make sense without reference to the attachments.

Conclusion: Having shown how you reasoned the problem through, state your conclusion. The conclusion must provide a complete, workable solution to the problem. The conclusion is nothing more than a brief restatement of the best possible solution or solutions which have been described in detail in the discussion. However, the conclusion should not continue the discussion. The conclusion should completely satisfy the requirements of the problem; it should never introduce new material.

Action Recommended: This part tells the reader what action should be taken. What recommendations you make depend upon your position in relation to the person receiving the study and upon the variables of the problem. The number of recommendations is not important; just be sure you have completed staff action.

Word the recommendations so that your superior, if he approves, need only sign them into action. Alternative recommendations should not be made. This does not mean that you cannot consider alternative solutions in the "Discussion." It does mean that, in recommending action, you commit yourself to the line of action you judge best. When staff work is completed, the section (bureau) head or chief is relieved of the research and study necessary to decide among several alternative courses of action.

You should include as attachments all directives necessary to support the actions recommended.

Ending Of The Staff Study Report: The ending should be simple and follow the format previously listed. The ending contains:
    1. The signature and title of the person or persons responsible for the report.
    2. Listing of attachments.

5. Completed Staff Work

A staff study report should represent completed staff work. This means that the government worker has solved a problem and presented a complete solution to his superior. The solution should be complete enough that all the superior or chief has to do is approve or disapprove.

When you submit a staff study, enclose in attachments the directives needed to put your plan to work. If a regulation or other form of instruction is needed, write it. Completed staff work will:
    1. Protect the chief from "half-baked" ideas, voluminous written reports and immature oral explanations.
    2. Allow the chief more time to do the things that only he can do.
    3. Provide the management intern who has real ideas a better chance to get a hearing.

The final test for completed staff work is this: If you were chief, would you be willing to stake your professional reputation on this staff study? If the answer is no, take it back and start over. It is not yet completed staff work.

6. The Technical Report

Your work on a technical problem is not finished when you find the solution. Why? Because your findings are valuable only when others can understand and use them.

Many technical groups are guilty of using shoptalk too liberally. If your audience is thoroughly familiar with your brand of shoptalk, it serves as a form of shorthand. Chances are, however, that your report will go beyond your immediate supervisor and leave your particular area of work. If this happens, the use of loosely defined technical terms may cause difficulty for the reader.

The technical man may write a report which is intended to be read by others of the organization or, at most, by other technical men who are familiar with the subject. This type of report is primarily for the record. Emphasis is put on the complete presentation of the facts; their interpretation is left almost entirely to the reader.

Frequently, however, the technical man must write a report to influence others. If you must prepare such a report, you have to satisfy not one but several readers of varying backgrounds. If you are writing for the busy chief – interested only in the highlights of the findings – a short, concise statement of the problem, the conclusions arrived at, and the recommendations may be all that are necessary. If you are writing for your immediate supervisor or a technical man in the chain of readers, you may have to give more detailed information.

For these reasons, the following form is usually recommended for the technical report:

1. Title page
2. Synopsis or abstract (a very brief statement of the problem, details of investigation, conclusions, and recommendations)
3. Table of contents (or outline)
4. List of tables and illustrations
5. A complete introduction (statement of the problem)
6*. Conclusions and recommendations
7. Body of the report (systematically organized with headings)
8*. Conclusions (final comment)
9. Attachments for detailed data (charts, graphs, tables, etc.)

*Note: Parts 6 and 8 may be combined and placed in sequence as part 6.

As you can see, the busy chief can read just the synopsis (part 2) or your complete introduction and statement of conclusions and recommendations (parts 5 and 6) and have enough information upon which to base his judgment. He can then depend upon members of his staff to check the complete report for accuracy and completeness.

Illustrations: Illustrations are always helpful to the reader of a technical report. You need to know how to plan them and make the most of them. Remember that a complex report presented without illustrations of any kind tends to become a bewildering mass of words.

Equations: In a technical report you may need to include equations. If you do, the following illustration shows how to set them up. The equation is followed immediately by a number in parentheses to show that this equation is one of a series; the symbols of the equation are explained in a column below the equation itself; and the period is used only at the end of the last explanatory phrase.

The minimum frequency for induction hardening depends on stock diameter. Expressed in equation form: $F = 180 / r^2$ (1)

where F is the practical minimum frequency in cycles per second, r is the radius of the bar or cylinder in inches. This equation gives minimum practical frequency for surface layers heated by induction, but does not take into account the flow of heat by conduction to layers beneath.

Headings: The visible evidence of the organization of a report is the headings. They guide the reader rapidly through the report, showing him points where his interest is greatest. If you study the headlines in a newspaper, you will get some suggestions on how to write headings for a report.

BASIC FUNDAMENTALS OF REPORT WRITING

CONTENTS

INSTRUCTIONAL OBJECTIVES	1
CONTENT	1
Introduction	1
1. Types of Reports	
The Formal Report	1
The Informal Report	
The Semi-Formal Report	
2. Examples of Reports	2
School Setting	
The Formal Report	
The Semi-Formal Report	
The Informal Report	
Public Service Agencies	
Police Reporting	
Other Reporting Areas	
3. The Report Writer	4
4. Choosing Best Words	4
Use Proper Word for Intended Meaning	
Eliminate Slang in Reports	
5. Choosing Best Phrases	6
Don't Use Weasel Words	
Cliches to Avoid	
Don't Use Excess Wordage	
Don't Be Pompous	
6. Writing Sentences	8
Be Simple	
Keep Active	
Don't be Wordy	
7. Writing a Good Paragraph	10
Developing a Paragraph	
Paragraph Construction	
8. Special Word Forms	10
Using Numbers Correctly	
Using Abbreviations Correctly	
Using Contractions Correctly	
Using Capital Letters Correctly	
Using Punctuation Correctly	
The Comma	
The Semicolon	
The Colon	
9. Using the Dictionary in Report Writing	13
Dictionary Usage	
Dictionary Content	
Word Division	
10. Summation	14
STUDENT LEARNING ACTIVITIES	15
TEACHER MANAGEMENT ACTIVITIES	15
EVALUATION QUESTIONS	17

BASIC FUNDAMENTALS OF REPORT WRITING

INSTRUCTIONAL OBJECTIVES

1. Ability to understand how reports are used.
2. Ability to form an appreciation for the importance of effective report writing in public service occupations.
3. Ability to define and differentiate between the types of reports.
4. Ability to select the proper form for a report.
5. Ability to recognize the steps in preparing a good report.
6. Ability to demonstrate a knowledge of correct word usage and its importance in a report.
7. Ability to demonstrate the proper grammatical structure in report writing.
8. Ability to explain the importance of using a dictionary in report writing.

CONTENT

INTRODUCTION

A report is the communication of information in the most convenient form to someone who wants or needs it. It is difficult to overstate the importance of reports in our complex society today. They provide the data on which far-reaching decisions and policy are determined. A report that is not accurate or that is incomplete may cause the writer and the receiver misunderstanding, antagonism, and costly errors. Repeated errors in reports may well cost the writer his position.

Many of the reports that public service workers make are oral ones. However, the more important reports are always required to be in writing.

A report is always addressed to someone - the audience. The audience is usually a superior who needs the information to determine what action to take or what recommendations to pass ori to his superior. The good report writer analyzes the audience to which the report will be directed.

- Should the report be a formal document or should the report be an informal memo?

- How will the audience use the report?

- Will it be passed along to others in the organization, or people in other areas?

The report writer's answers to questions such as these may well determine the format that is selected for the report.

1. TYPES OF REPORTS

   <u>The Formal Report</u>. Formal reports usually follow a format prescribed by the agency or department. A central office typically supplies the form on which the report is to be prepared and submitted. A copy of a previous

report is frequently used as a guideline in preparing the new one. This procedure saves considerable time and makes it easier for the central office to analyze and interpret the information contained in the report.

The Informal Report. Another type of report, the informal one, frequently takes the form of a note or memo requesting additional supplies, services, or providing suggestions for the supervisor or a fellow worker. The informal report could possibly contain abbreviations, first names, and technical jargon that would be meaningless to anyone not acquainted with the situation in which it was written.

The Semi-Formal Report. A semi-formal report fits between the casual or informal memo and the highly structured and authoritative formal report. The semi-formal report is to be considered more important than the informal one and consequently is written with more thought and care than the informal report.

2. EXAMPLES OF REPORTS

   School Setting. The various types of reports may be illustrated in school settings:

   - *The Formal Report*. Progress reports, attendance reports, accident reports, and classroom reports prepared by students; these are all examples of well-structured formal reports. The importance of such reports is great. For example, the attendance reports determine how many teachers will be added or deleted from the faculty, in addition to being the basis for computing the state's financial contribution to the local school district.

   - *The Semi-Formal Report* is illustrated by the office referral requesting action because of a student's behavior. It may result in a student-administrator conference, a parent conference, or even student suspension from school.

   - *The Informal Report*. The note that a teacher leaves in the school mail for the staff assistant in charge of audiovisual equipment requesting service on the malfunctioning movie projector is an example of an informal report.

   Public Service Agencies. The public-service report writer will find that he is writing:

   - About specific subjects, and about various technicalities or events associated with the governmental agency or a responsibility assigned to it.

   - With certain formal elements, such as the technical vocabulary of the department and the use of forms prepared by the department or agency.

- With an attitude of impartiality and objectivity, taking extreme care to convey information accurately and concisely, and with no attempt to arouse emotions.

Police Reporting - An illustration which would be meaningful to students may be made by examining what a policeman would include in a report when investigating an automobile accident. The policeman's report must contain such specific facts as:

- The names, addresses, phone numbers, ages, drivers' license numbers, and the identification of witnesses to the accident.

- Where the accident occurred - address.

- Description of the accident scene.

- The witnesses' observations - obtaining not only their account of events, but from what point they observed the event, and what they were doing at the time.

- Time and day of the accident.

- Weather conditions at the time of accident.

- The location of traffic signals, stop signs, skid marks, traffic lanes, etc.

- Description of the injuries, If any, or lack of apparent injuries.

- Description of the automobiles involved and apparent damages.

The investigating officer will have a pad of accident report forms which will outline the information needed. This insures that in the emotion and tension of the accident scene the investigating officer will be reminded of the information that he needs to include in the report. Numbers will be used to code certain information. This speeds up the writing, simplifies the recording and filing of the information, and makes the report less emotional.

The accident report will be of major importance when the insurance companies settle the claim. If there is a dispute over the settlement, the police report will be entered into the court record. The officer who wrote the report will also have to testify. The testimony may not be called for years after the accident and the officer will have to use the report to refresh his memory. It would probably be difficult for the officer otherwise to recall all of the events or even to notice them all at the time, as he may have had to direct traffic, administer first aid, call an ambulance, and keep curious bystanders out of the way. Even though human life may have been lost or saved by the policeman's actions on the scene, the primary issues in which the court or insurance adjusters will be interested are the facts in his report.

Other Reporting Areas - There are other workers in the public service area, such as teachers' aides, recreation aides, and forestry aides, who are likely to be required to complete accident reports while on the job. While their reports may not be as sensational as the police report, they are important and may be used in subsequent litigation.

It should also be pointed out that any report may have far-reaching ramifications. However, it is wise to be especially careful if a financial settlement between two adversaries will be affected by the report.

3. THE REPORT WRITER

Regardless of the type of report that is being prepared, the key to a good report is a good writer. The writer is the prime mover of the entire process. He gathers the material, interprets it, organizes it, and chooses the vocabulary. The writer imposes meaning merely by determining whether to make the report a formal, a semi-formal, or an informal one.

The reader is led to an understanding by an orderly presentation of the facts. The facts are determined by the writer's examination and observations of the situation or activity. The report's validity hinges upon the competence and objectivity of the writer and the accuracy of his observations.

Competence in report writing means that an individual has acquired the technique of careful inquiry. This may be illustrated by the police officer at the scene of the accident. He will take statements from witnesses, take measurements of skid marks, inspect and record the automobiles' registrations, and inspect the scene of the accident for real evidence that may have been instrumental in the cause of the accident, such as flat tires, conditions of the tires on the automobiles, mechanical defects, health of the drivers, etc. The report writer must acquire the habit of orderly thinking from problems to solutions, and learn to write an exact statement.

A good report communicates deaf ideas in simple language. The organization is orderly and fast moving. It is easy to read and uses visual aids where they will best carry forward the message. These skills are required of almost every member of governmental agencies. Management quickly recognizes competence in the preparation of reports. The individual who writes them well will assume a position of leadership at every level where accurate data supplies the basis for a difficult decision.

4. CHOOSING BEST WORDS

A major aspect of clear and concise report writing is being careful to select the proper word to express the thought exactly.

Use Proper Word for Intended Meaning. Since any one word may have a number of different meanings in different contexts, the writer must be certain that the word chosen is appropriate to convey the intended meaning within the human situation in which it is used. Paul Douglas, in his book

Communicating Through Reports, illustrates this point with "word." He lists twelve different meanings, ranging from the preacher expounding the *Word* (scripture) to the wife's having the *last word* (decision). This relationship of meaning to the environment and circumstances of its use is known as *context*.

Nearly all words mean more than they seem to mean; they possess associative meanings, almost outlying areas of suggestive values. The bare dictionary meaning of a word is its *denotation*. The *connotation* of a word relates to the suggestions and associations which have surrounded it.

For example, a dictionary definition of the word "gold" is "a precious yellow metal which is highly malleable and ductible. This is its denotation. But along with its denotative meaning, gold has also been associated with wealth, value, color, and power. These characteristics are the connotations of gold.

Beyond the core of the dictionary definition are suggestions, associations, and implications. Connotations must be watched as they have practical consequences for the report writer. Words and phrases with unpleasant connotations may become fighting words which blind the reader to anything else in the report. The following words are a few that have negative suggestions: mistakes, inefficient, death, refuse, error, rejecting, prohibited, unfair, poor judgment, and failed.

The writer may avoid irritation by choosing words with positive or neutral connotations. Note the difference in meaning of the following words:

- car, automobile, limousine
- inebriated, intoxicated, drunk
- portly, stout, obese
- smell, smell bad, stink
- slow, lazy, sluggish
- firm, obstinate, pigheaded
- Negro, colored man, black man
- dog, hound, mongrel

To use words both accurately and effectively, one must understand their connotations as well as their denotations. Social welfare aides, employment service workers, and probation services aides need to be especially alert to those words which are unique to the groups of people they serve. When wishing to express something with literal accuracy, the report writer will rely wholly upon the standards set by the department or dictionary definitions.

<u>Eliminate Slang in Reports</u>. *Slang should not be used in reports except when reporting dialogue.* There are several reasons for not using slang:

- First, many slang words and expressions are so short-lived that they will be outmoded before the report will have lived its useful life.

o Second, the use of slang expressions may be an excuse for not searching for the exact words to express the meaning.

Many slang expressions are only rubber stamps; to refer to a person as a "dude" hardly expresses exactly any critical judgment or intelligent description. To argue that such a word conveys precisely the intended meaning is to reveal a poverty of vocabulary, or careless thinking and laxness. The most serious charge against slang is that it becomes a substitute for thinking. Public service workers are likely to encounter the following slang:

- o grubby
- o get burned
- o the boss
- o real cool dude
- o far out
- o right on
- o groovy

- o bummer
- o a drag
- o rip off
- o split
- o low rider
- o doing your own thing
- o busted

The list could go on indefinitely. It would be very difficult to get a widely acceptable definition for any one of the above slang words. *Slang does express feeling, but when writing reports, the main concern is facts, not feelings.*

5. <u>CHOOSING BEST PHRASES</u>

<u>Don't Use Weasel Words</u>. Other words to avoid in writing reports are what some authors call "weasel words." *A weasel word is a phrase that rids the writer of any responsibility for a statement.* By the use of the weasel word, the writer attempts to wriggle out of a position of accountability for an observation, inference, or statement, as may be seen by these examples:

- o It would be difficult to estimate ...

- o It is too early to say whether ...

- o It is generally believed that ...

- o It would appear that ...

- o There may be a tendency toward ...

Weasel words are usually used with the passive voice, which is discussed later in this unit under "Writing Sentences."

<u>Clichés to Avoid</u>. Public-service workers, like many other report writers, too often use words and phrases which are trite, outworn, commonplace, and flat stereotypes. Here are some examples of cliches which should be avoided:

- o It certainly merits study ...

- We will see what may be done ...

- This suggestion certainly has merit ...
- The matter is receiving our closest attention ...
- We will explore every avenue ...
- The handwriting on the wall ...
- Let's get down to brass tacks ...
- Naturally, the child's interest is our concern ...
- Fools rush in ...
- In the last analysis ...
- No thinking man ...
- The skeleton in the closet ...
- Let sleeping dogs ...

Cliches are similar to slang in that they are but rubber stamps, "stereotyped plates" of thought and expression. They save the writer the trouble of thinking exactly what he means. Consequently, they get in the way of clear and concise report writing.

<u>Don't Use Excess Wordage</u>. Diction, to be effective, must be as economical as possible. Necessary words should not be omitted nor should the report be sketchy. However, wordiness should be avoided as it lessens the force of expression. *In forceful writing, the ratio of ideas to words is high.* Conciseness alone will not achieve effective writing, but it is extremely difficult to write forcefully if you use two or three words to convey the idea which one word would express. Note these examples of excess or "superfluous" words:

- absolutely parallel
- first beginnings
- free gratis
- someone I met up with
- perfect circle
- the sunset in the west
- resume again
- join together

<u>Don't be Pompous</u>. When it is possible to reduce a group of words to a single word, it should be done. Here are some examples of economy in diction that are achieved by reducing pompous phrases to more natural words:

<u>Pompous</u>	<u>Natural</u>
in the nature of	like
for the purpose of	for
prior to	before
subsequent to	after
despite the fact that	though
give consideration to	consider
give instruction to	instruct
is due in large measure to	is due largely to
confidential nature	confidential information

6. WRITING SENTENCES

Be Simple. One of the most important rules to follow in writing a report is to keep your sentences short, usually twenty words or less. Language, like a machine, will be the most efficient when it operates on the principle that the more simple and better arranged the parts, the greater the effect which is produced. The subject-verb-object sentence is the best arrangement of parts in the simple report.

Keep Active. Verbs should be kept active. Avoid the passive voice; this puts excess words in a sentence, and its dullness derives as much from its extra wordage as from its impersonality. John was hit by Don says no more than Don hit John but takes 66 percent more words.

The passive voice's inevitable "was" and "by" do nothing but connect; worse, all the "was's" and "by's" and "has been's" actually get in the way of words carrying the meaning. It's like underbrush, it slows you down and hides what the report reader should see.

The passive voice, in its wordiness, is likely to be unclear even on the surface. When it eliminates the subject of the verb, as it usually does, it is intrinsically unclear. For example, a sentence written in the passive voice will often begin: "This evidence has been selected because...." The reader cannot tell who did the selecting. Does the writer mean that he picked it or does he describe some process of popular selection? It is usually surmised that the writer did the selecting, but why doesn't he say so and save a word and avoid confusion? "I selected this evidence because...." *The report writer should be careful not to leave the reader with any assumptions or implications.*

Don't be Wordy. Government writing is often noted for its wordiness. The following example is taken from a World War II price control regulation:

"Ultimate consumer means a person or group of persons, generally constituting a domestic household, who purchase eggs generally at the individual stores or retailers or purchase and receive deliveries of eggs at the place of abode of the individual or domestic household from producers or retail route sellers and who use such eggs for their consumption or food." This statement may be changed, without changing its meaning, by reducing it to:

"Ultimate consumers are people who buy eggs to eat them."

A good writer sees sharply what he wants to say, says directly what he sees, edits what he says, and takes pain to ease his reader's task. The example just given illustrates how much more readable a short sentence is than a long one.

7. WRITING A GOOD PARAGRAPH

The next major step after writing sentences is the construction of paragraphs. A good paragraph will clearly state the central ideas, it will fill in supporting details, and show how the central idea relates to the ideas which precede and follow it. The proper length of a paragraph is much like Abraham Lincoln's idea of a speech; it should be long enough to reach the end. There are exceptions, however. A report writer should be critical of his writing when a page of typewritten copy contains more than three or less than one complete paragraph.

Developing a Paragraph. There are many different ways of developing a paragraph in a report. The entry-level public-service worker may well utilize a variation of the following patterns of development:

- *Definition and description*. The writer gives his reader al1 the concepts he needs to follow the presentation.

- *Historical summary*. The writer briefs the reader on where the problem came from and why it is a problem. It provides a perspective for the problem.

- *Case history*. The report writer details an actual record for the reader.

- *Description of a process*. The report describes in detail how factors work together to produce a certain result.

- *Occasional summary*. The writer restates the essential data and ties facts together to clarify them for the reader.

- *Cause and effect*. The writer explains the forces that pro-duce certain consequences.

- *Examination of alternatives*. The writer may present the material so that the reader can make an examination of alternatives and their possible consequences.

- *Directive*. The reader will be told what to do. The writer may describe steps to be taken.

Paragraph Construction. Regardless of the paragraph's development, a well-constructed paragraph will be correct, clear, and effective. Eight desirable paragraph characteristics are listed below:

- A good paragraph contains an implied or expressed topic sentence.

- A good paragraph is never sketchy or incomplete. It contains a complete body of thought.

- A good paragraph is mechanically correct. It is properly indented or otherwise set off. It correctly represents every change of speaker in dialogue.

- A good paragraph is unified. Extraneous details are eliminated.

- A good paragraph contains material arranged in proper order. Good arrangement of ideas demonstrates logical thinking on the part of the writer.

- A good paragraph should make orderly clear progress and there should be clear passage from one paragraph to another.

- A good paragraph will be of suitable length.

- A good paragraph is well proportioned to the importance of the content. The longest paragraph of the report should not deal with the least significant idea.

8. <u>SPECIAL WORD FORMS</u>

The report writer will need to know how to handle such other items as abbreviations and numbers, in addition to writing clear sentences in well constructed paragraphs.

<u>Using Numbers Correctly</u>. Nearly all reports contain numbers. Should the number be written out or should it be shown in figures? Many reports consist primarily of numbers. Such reports call for the use of figures. However, other reports which are not primarily numerical reports may leave the writer in doubt as to how the numbers should be shown. The following suggestions may be helpful:

- Numbers requiring the use of more than one word or a hyphenated word are usually written as figures.

- A number which begins a sentence is written as a word; if this is awkward or inconsistent with the rest of the text, replace the sentence.

- Numbers under ten are usually written as words unless they appear in writing which is full of numbers.

- Numbers that express dimensions are usually written as figures.

- Numbers which contain decimal fractions are always written as figures.

- Any number naming a common fraction is usually written as a hyphenated word.
- Numbers in any sentence in which other numbers are to occur in figure form are usually written in figures.

- Numbers that tell either time, date, or percentage are usually written in figures.

- Numbers above ten naming streets are usually written as figures with the indicators of pronounciation, -st, -nd, -th, attached.

- Round numbers, such as "thousands," are usually written as words except where numbers are occurring very frequently.

- Any number appearing occasionally and simple enough to express in one word is usually written as a word.

- Numbers appearing as two separate categories, one after the other, are usually written as words for the first category and as figures for the second. (five 2x4 boards)

The report writer should remember that the above guidelines are suggestions and that some of them may actually contradict each other. Common sense should determine whether or not a number be written as a figure or a word.

Using Abbreviations Correctly. Abbreviations are found more often in reports than in any other form of writing. Although the use of abbreviations is a healthy part of the style of field reports, it is definitely limited and kept in check by both tradition and common sense. *Only those abbreviations which will be easily understood by the reader are to be used.* Many agencies or departments will have a number of abbreviations that they use regularly, particularly in informal reports. Handbooks or manuals issued by the department will list these and the new worker should memorize them. The use of abbreviations has met with limited success because of the time saved in writing certain reports; the use should be very restricted in formal reports.

There are several rules regarding the general idea of permissible abbreviations in report writing:

- Whenever abbreviations have been used so long that they have assumed vocabulary status, they should be used. Some such abbreviations are Mr., Mrs., B.C., A.D., FBI, CIA, a.m., p.m. (Each job family will have a number of abbreviations of its own.)
- Whenever the names of units are preceded by numerals, it is usually best to abbreviate the names of the units. For instance:

    a. The auto was going 75-mph in the 25-mph zone.
    b. It was 65° F today.
    c. The unit has a 3-hp engine.

- If an abbreviation makes an English word (as for example, in. for inches), use a period. Otherwise, most good writers do <u>not</u> use periods in <u>most</u> cases.

If a term must be repeated many times in a report, that term calls for explanation and thereafter possible abbreviation, regardless of what it is.

Using Contractions Correctly. A contraction is a form of abbreviation. It is a word written with an apostrophe to indicate the omission of a letter. Contractions should be used very seldom in formal reports, but are common in semiformal and informal ones. Field reports are full of abbreviations and contractions as their use can greatly speed up the process of gathering data in the field.

Using Capital Letters Correctly. Report writing calls for no departure from the conventional rules for the use of capital letters. Proper names, names of cities and states, official titles, and organizations are always captalized. There are two practices common to reports:

- Capitalize all important words in titles, division headings, side headings, and captions. By "important" is meant all words except articles, prepositions, and conjunctions.

- Capitalize Figure, Table, Volume, Number as part of titles. Thus, reference would be made to Figure 4, Table 2, etc.

When in doubt, do not capitalize.

Using Punctuation Correctly. Clear communication is dependent upon yet another aspect of written language, punctuation. Every sentence begins with a capital letter, and ends with either a period, question mark, or exclamation point. Punctuation which does not contribute to the clarity of thought should be avoided. Most of the difficulties with punctuation arise out of the use of the comma, semicolon, and colon. For information on other punctuation, see any good handbook of grammar.

The Comma. The principal uses of the comma are:

- Between independent clauses connected by a coordinating conjunction (and, but, for, or, nor, yet). But if commas are used in any of the independent clauses constituting a sentence, a semicolon must be used between the clauses.

- After introductory clauses or phrases preceding the main clause of the sentence.

- Between items in a series.

- Around parenthetical phrases, appositives, and nonrestric-tive modifiers.

The Semicolon. The semicolon is almost as strong a mark of separation as the period. It is chiefly used between the independent clauses not connected with one of the coordinating conjunctions, and between clauses connected with a coordinating conjunction which are long, or unrelated, or contain commas.

The Colon. The colon signals that something is to follow. It is a mark introducing lists, series, and quotations. It is used as a salutation in a business letter, in separating the hours and minutes in a statement of time, or in separating volume and pages in a bibliographical entry.

9. <u>USING THE DICTIONARY IN REPORT WRITING</u>

<u>Dictionary Usage</u>. The report writer should be aware of the fact that most dictionaries have a section listing the principal rules of capitalization, punctuation, and spelling. A dictionary should be considered one of the necessary tools for good report writing, together with the pencil and paper. The report writer should be using the dictionary for the following purposes:

o To determine the exact meaning of a word.

o To determine the correct spelling.

o To determine whether or not a word should be capitalized.

o To determine how a word should be divided at the end of a line.

o To determine correct pronunciation.

o To determine whether or not a hyphen should be used in a compound word.

<u>Dictionary Content</u>. In addition, the dictionary also has a list of common foreign words and phrases. It is obvious that much of the material that a report writer must master is to be found in a dictionary. The excellent report writer has the ability to select the exact word. No one can buy, sell, write letters, use the telephone, give orders, make a speech, or prepare a report, except by using words. Everything else being equal, the individual who knows the most about words will be the most successful in his occupation. *To develop the mastery of language necessary to use the exact word, the writer must know how to use the dictionary skillfully and he must use it frequently.*

The dictionary is a tool that will always be needed by the educated person. As a matter of fact, the better educated a person is, the more likely he is to refer frequently to a dictionary.

<u>Word Division</u>. One use of the dictionary mentioned above is for determining the correct place to divide a word at the end of a line. Since more errors are made in dividing words at the end of a line than in spelling them, capitalizing them, or in using them, it is important that the report writer learn to divide words correctly. Below are eight rules for dividing words at the end of a line:

o Never divide a word of one syllable.

o Do not divide a word of four letters.

- A one-letter syllable at the beginning of a word, or a one or two-letter syllable at the end of a word must not be separated from the rest of the word. (Examples: "about" not "a-bout"; "ready" not "read-y.")

- When a word containing three or more syllables is to be divided at a one-letter syllable, the one-letter syllable should be written on the first line rather than on the second. (Example: "maga-zine" not "mag-azine.")

- When a word is to be divided at a point where two vowels that are pronounced separately come together, these vowels should be divided into separate syllables. (Example: "continu-ation" not "continua-tion.") Note that this rule is an exception to the one stated above.

- A syllable that does not contain a vowel must not be separated from the remainder of the word. (Example: "wouldn't" not "would-n't.")

- Avoid dividing hyphenated words, such as "self-conscious," except at the hyphen.

- When a final consonant is doubled before a suffix, the additional consonant should be placed with the suffix. (Example: "run-ning" not "runn-ing.")

When in doubt about the proper syllable makeup of a word, consult the dictionary. Do not guess at the division of a word.

10. <u>SUMMATION</u>

English grammar essentials, such as correct punctuation, capitalization, syllabication, and correct use of numbers and abbreviations, are all part of the skills that the successful report writer has at his disposal. The beginning public-service worker is well advised to obtain a list of the words that appear frequently in his job family, or are a part of the technical or professional vocabulary, and memorize them. Common report forms should be reviewed and used as a guide for making observations and examinations of data when preparing to write a report. The writer may find that maps are needed to show geographical location, charts to visualize statistical data, or tables to determine relationships. Clarity will be the guide dictating how any idea may best be communicated to the reader.

In conclusion, the report writer must know what details to look for, must select the proper format for the report, must select the best possible words that do not have any emotional connotations and build them into short, effective sentences. Paragraphs must be developed by the writer around the central thoughts, leaving nothing to be imagined by the reader. The importance of word relationship and idea sequence is crucial.

Remember, a report is written to express an idea, not to impress a superior.

15

STUDENT LEARNING ACTIVITIES	○ Write a report explaining a career choice.
	○ View the six films trips, *Constructing Reports,* and evaluate the information they contain.
	○ Complete the matching vocabulary exercise prepared by the teacher for the occupation group selected by the student.
	○ Demonstrate a knowledge of the active and passive verbs in report writing by changing a report prepared by the teacher from the passive voice to the active.
	○ List three words having unfavorable connotations and explain how they could be particularly embarrassing to the writer.
	○ Identify the type of paragraph development used in each of the paragraphs which the teacher has prepared.
	○ Keep a notebook for discussion notes and class handouts.
	○ Take a diagnostic test, and complete remedial lessons, if needed, on punctuation and capitalization.
	○ Complete a dictionary assignment.
	○ Prepare reports describing the events in a simulated classroom interruption.
	○ Prepare a group report on the students' attendance in class, citing the percentage of absentees each day. Compare Monday to Tuesday, etc., and list the frequency of reasons for the absences.
	○ Evaluate the reports prepared by the class members in the above two activities.
TEACHER MANAGEMENT ACTIVITIES	○ Prepare a bulletin board display illustrating the components of a good report.
	○ Review the materials in the local audiovisual library to locate teaching aids that are readily available.
	○ Make arrangements for showing the movie, *Writing a Good Paragraph.*
	○ Make arrangements to show the filmstrips in the series: *Constructing Reports.* (6 filmstrips)
	○ Prepare discussion notes on the types of reports, and the importance and purpose of each type.
	○ Collect examples of reports from the eight job families in the Public Service Occupation area.

- Prepare a vocabulary list of technical and professional words from each of the public-service entry-level job families.

- Prepare matching exercises for the vocabulary words and their definitions for each of the major job groups.

- Prepare overlays for use with an overhead projector illustrating good and bad reports.

- Prepare a list of sentences containing passive-voice verbs which the students are to change to active verbs.

- Prepare a discussion of word meanings and emphasize the importance of connotation.

- Obtain or write, and present, paragraphs illustrating the seven ways of developing a paragraph.

- Plan simulated situations from which the students will have to prepare reports.

- Prepare a handout for students containing suggestions for the use of numbers in reports.

- Prepare discussion notes for the use of abbreviations in reports.

- Prepare a diagnostic quiz on punctuation marks and capitalization.

- Discuss and test the use of the dictionary in the classroom.

- Prepare a student handout on the eight rules for dividing words at the end of a line.

EVALUATION QUESTIONS
Basic Report Writing

1. Public service workers are likely to write:

   A. Formal reports
   B. Informal reports
   C. Semi-formal reports
   D. All of the above

2. Which statement is untrue?

   A. A good report writer does not have to be exact about facts
   B. A good report writer writes objectively and accurately about his observations
   C. A good report writer uses visual aids where they will help put over the message
   D. A good report writer gathers his material in an orderly way

3. Police reports are important because:

   A. They help settle arguments
   B. They help refresh the officer's memory
   C. Financial settlements may be involved
   D. All of the above

4. Which statement is not true?

   A. A good paragraph contains materials arranged in random order
   B. The length of the paragraph is suited to its importance
   C. A good paragraph is mechanically correct - indented or set off
   D. A good paragraph should make orderly, clear passage from one paragraph to another

5. A good paragraph should:

   A. Include all minor details
   B. Contain a topic sentence
   C. Leave out the main ideas
   D. Leave out the important details

6. Inaccurate and incomplete reports can cause:

   A. Misunderstanding
   B. Anger
   C. Costly errors
   D. All of the above

7. Writers do not refer to dictionaries when they need to know: 7.____

   A. Correct spelling
   B. How a word should be divided
   C. Detailed information about a subject
   D. Whether a hyphen should be used

8. Good report writers use: 8.____

   A. Slang as much as possible
   B. Words with unpleasant meanings
   C. Phrases that rid the writer of responsibility
   D. None of the above

9. When writing a report, it is best to use: 9.____

   A. Phrases that are used over and over
   B. Short, simple sentences
   C. As many words as possible
   D. An inactive tone

10. Which statement is incorrect? 10.____

    A. A number which begins a sentence is written as a figure
    B. Numbers under ten are usually written as words
    C. Numbers requiring the use of more than one word are usually written as figures
    D. Numbers which contain decimal fractions are always written as figures

11. Contractions are seldom used in: 11.____

    A. Field reports
    B. Semi-formal reports
    C. Formal reports
    D. Informal reports

12. Titles and the names of organizations are: 12.____

    A. Never capitalized
    B. Not capitalized in informal reports
    C. Sometimes capitalized in formal reports
    D. Always capitalized

13. After introductory clauses or phrases, one should use: 13.____

    A. A period
    B. A comma
    C. A question mark
    D. An exclamation mark

14. Between long, unrelated clauses that are connected with a conjunction, one should use: 14.____

    A. A period
    B. A question mark
    C. A semi-colon
    D. A colon

KEY (CORRECT ANSWERS)

1. D
2. A
3. D
4. A
5. B

6. D
7. C
8. D
9. B
10. A

11. C
12. D
13. B
14. C

THE NARRATIVE REPORT

CONTENTS

	Page
I. COMPILING THE DATA	1
II. ORGANIZING MATERIALS	2
III. WRITING THE REPORT	5

The Narrative Report

The narrative report is to an establishment what an introductory statement is to a definition. A good narrative report provides the context in which the particular study was made and serves to orient the reader to the circumstances under which jobs existed at that time. This background information is especially important to the reader before he examines the individual job analysis schedules. Further, the narrative report provides broad general occupational and industrial information which cannot be properly included in the job analysis schedule.

I. COMPILING THE DATA

The information in a narrative report grows out of discussions with workers, plant officials, industry experts, college or technical school personnel, and review of the technical literature pertaining to the industry. The analyst makes inquiries concerning the structure or organization of the establishment, the job interrelationships, the work flow processes, personnel policies and practices, hazards, and any other items which he feels will contribute to the job information. Much of this information can be obtained during the orientation tour, discussed in chapter III.

Examples of the kind of questions for which the analyst should seek answers are:

1. (If industrial) What is the purpose of the establishment? What are the processes by which raw materials are converted to finished products? (If non-industrial) What is the nature of the service rendered? What knowledge or technologies are required for adequate performance? How is the service rendered? What are the general duties or procedures?

2. What are the general environmental conditions? What are the hazards encountered by workers? What working conditions are peculiar to the establishment?

3. Are the services or work flow of the establishment divided into departments or units, and if so, how? How are these units interrelated, or how are they arranged in a work flow process?

4. What are the personnel practices? Are women used in other than traditional clerical jobs? Are minorities, handicapped, or older workers employed; if so, in what types of jobs? What is the trend in regard to such workers? Does a form of career lattice exist in this establishment? What are the entry jobs? Are training courses provided by the establishment?

5. Does this establishment have any unique characteristics in comparison to all other establishments in the industry? What is the history of the development of the establishment? Has it automated or initiated any progressive or unusual processes, equipment, or services? What effects have these new ideas or machinery had on the activities and employment status of the establishment?

I. ORGANIZING MATERIALS

Generally, the data obtained through the discussions with establishment personnel or other technical experts will fall fairly obviously under several major headings. Liberal use of such headings and their subheadings, even in a very short report provides the reader with a ready reference to the particular sections of the report and an easier to read, more interesting text. In addition, the use of headings helps the analyst to organize his materials in terms of the headings and helps him set limits on the amount of information included in the narrative.

A standard formula for organizing the report is neither possible nor desirable, as each report and each analyst's presentation will include many different types of data. However, a few general headings have been found to be significant in most reports. The outline below presents these headings, with typical items explained in the contents. A report may not include all these headings, or it may include additional or other headings. These general headings are:

Introduction or purpose of establishment
    Purpose
    Scope and/or limit of study
    History and/or development of the establishment

Environmental Conditions
    Description of layout
    Description of equipment
    General environmental conditions and general working conditions

Organization and Operations or Activities
    Departmentalization of establishment
    Work flow
    Processes (if industrial)
    Services (if non-industrial)

Personnel Policies and Practices
    Hiring requirements
    Recruitment and/or sources of workers
    Methods of training
    Hiring of minorities, handicapped and disadvantaged
    Entry jobs
    Career lattices and/or promotional opportunities
    Job restructuring
    Effects of automation on personnel

Other Section (s)
    Comments
    Effects of automation on establishment or industry
    Appendix and Glossary

Introduction or Purpose of the Establishment

The section under this heading should begin with a statement of the product or service of the establishment. If the study is in an industrial plant, this section would include a general discussion of the raw materials involved, the processes used, and the range and variety of products produced. If a non-industrial establishment is studied, the section would include a description of the nature of the service, and to whom and how the service is rendered. The name of the establishment does not appear on the report, which is identified by the establishment number only. This number appears at the top of the first page immediately beneath the words, Narrative Report.

Frequently, this section also includes a history of the establishment; what it began as, how it developed, and possibly some future plans of the establishment or future trends in the industry if these are significant to the employment status.

Any restrictions which the employer may impose on the study (such as processes which he wishes to keep secret) and which therefore affect the preparation of job analysis schedules could be noted here.

Environmental Conditions

This section would include a description of the layout of the establishment, complete with size, to give the reader a picture of the physical arrangement of buildings, facilities, equipment, storage, or related areas as they affect work flow. The narration in this section would also include information on equipment, machines, and/or tools used, and working conditions. The description given here should be concerned with the overall establishment picture and should furnish information not contained in the individual job analysis schedules.

Organization and Activities

An explanation of the organization of the establishment gives the necessary orientation for reading the individual schedules. This section might begin with a discussion of the units, processes or major activities, and with their interrelation or position in the work flow. This would then be followed by a breakdown of the units, processes, or activities into separate subheadings with more detailed descriptions of each. When this section is read in conjunction with the environmental conditions section, it should enable the reader to visualize the total work situation into which the worker fits.

Personnel Policies and Practices

Here the analyst would give a picture of the establishment's hiring requirements and its methods of placement. Included under this heading are educational, physical, and other requirements; the employer's methods of recruitment; and his policy and practice in hiring members of special groups. In addition, subheadings deal with methods of entry and training given by or sanctioned by the establishment, and career lattices or other promotional opportunities which exist in the establishment.

If the purpose of the study is to find job worker situations which could be restructured, or if the establishment has practiced some form of job restructuring, a discussion of this should appear here. Also, if the establishment has become automated and the automation has had significant impact on its employment, a subheading devoted to this should appear here. In either case, the discussion describes the effects of restructuring or automation on placement policies and practices, on employment statistics, and the resultant changes in educational and training requirements.

The following questions can serve as guides to the analyst for obtaining pertinent data:

Related to employment of women: What openings for women are there in this establishment? Are there environmental factors which negate successful employment? What is the establishment's attitude toward their employment? Have jobs been restructured to facilitate their employment?

Related to employment of the handicapped: Where and in what types of work are they employed? Is the establishment planning to accelerate the hiring of this type of worker? Has the possibility of restructuring jobs for them been considered?

Related to employment of members of minority groups: Are there limits to employment of these workers? To their promotional opportunities? Are there jobs or units in the establishment where minority workers are not employed? What is the employment trend in the~ hiring of these workers?

Related to employment of the disadvantaged worker: Does the establishment employ any less-than-fully qualified persons, or persons who qualify as disadvantaged? Has the establishment made any provision for special training for these workers? If not, could any jobs in the establishment be performed by a disadvantaged worker?

Related to training: Is there a formal in plant training program? Are there outside facilities to which the establishment has recourse? Are there formal apprenticeships in effect?

Related to career lattices: Is there a formally established career lattice in the establishment? Are there well defined lines of promotion and transfer? Are in-step and on the-job training programs integrated into this lattice? What are the entry occupations? What proportion of jobs in the establishment are entry occupations? Does the establishment participate in Federal training programs?

Related to job restructuring: Has this establishment tried any formal job restructuring? If not, could the jobs in this establishment be restructured? Are there factors which limit this possibility? What have been or what could be the results of restructuring in employment status? Has or could job restructuring create new or more entry occupations, and establish more meaningful career lattices?

Other Section (s)

Sometimes a report will include a section or sections devoted to special or unique topics.

For example, the analyst may include a section concerned with the product market, or special factors affecting work flow in the establishment. The discussion of the history of the establishment.

or of future trends in the establishment or the industry may appear here rather than in the introduction or purpose of the establishment section.

A special case in this section is that concerned with the effects of automation or mechanization in an industry or establishment. In these instances a discussion of the effects of automation on personnel should appear in the personnel policies and practices section, and all other aspects of automation or mechanization, i.e., changes in equipment, changes in processes or activities, effects on working conditions and physical requirements, would be included in a special section at the end of the narrative report.

Appendix and Glossary

In the course of his study, the analyst may obtain from management or other sources supplemental materials such as brochures or forms, which might add additional interest and information to the report. These should be included as an appendix. The analyst may also find certain technical terms, processes, or equipment which he feels need to be clarified for the reader. These should appear in a glossary at the end of the report.

III WRITING THE REPORT

Writing a narrative report is the process of converting the information secured into useable reference material. The report will present only pertinent and essential information in the fewest words consistent with clarity, proper arrangement for exposition, and accuracy of word usage.

Note: The SIC Code(s) which is identical to that entered on the staffing schedule should be entered on page one of the Narrative Report.

GUIDELINES FOR REPORT WRITING

1. The analyst should distinguish clearly between statements based on fact and those based on his own or other's opinions. At times, statements of Opinions enhance the value of the narrative by rendering an overall picture of the study. However, the source of statements of opinion should be identified as, "In the analyst's opinion" or "The personnel manager states ...." Crediting a statement thus, while indicating that the statement is not substantiated completely, gives authority for the opinion and lends weight to it.

2. A paragraph must be built around one central thought, and sentences not contributing to that specific thought do not belong in the paragraph. However, breaks between paragraphs serve as resting points for the reader, and paragraphs of more than 200 or so words should not be used.

3. Suitable transition statements are necessary for the reader to follow the changing thought from paragraph to paragraph. Even when main headings and subheadings are used, the transition should be such that the reader understands that he has completed one thought and is progressing to the next.

4. Because of its position of emphasis, the opening sentence often is used to state the central thought which the remainder of the paragraph expands and supports. At other times it points the direction in which the new paragraph will move away from the preceding paragraph. The emphatic position of this first sentence in a paragraph, as well as the last sentence, should not be wasted by the writer.

5. The main headings may be centered and underlined. Secondary headings then can be placed at the left margin and underlined. Third-order headings (usually to be avoided) might be placed in the text and underlined. "Label" headings should be avoided. For example, while "Plant Environmental Factors" is adequate for a very broad heading, a subheading under it should say: "Physical Layout of Departments," rather than "Layouts." The format should be consistent.

An example of a narrative report follows.

EXAMPLE

NARRATIVE REPORT

SIC-2281

Establishment No. 360-150-392

Purpose of Establishment

This establishment is a processing plant within a synthetic yarn-producing division of a yarn and thread manufacturing corporation. It is engaged in spinning yarn from man-made fibers for use in manufacturing such articles as hosiery, pile fabrics, and men's and women's outerwear. Basic yarn counts produced range from <u>6's</u> to <u>30's</u> both single and plied.

Prior to 1959 this plant was engaged in the manufacture of carded cotton knitting yarns of coarse to medium count. The transition to producing synthetic yarns was completed in early 1959 with the installation of machinery developed for manufacturing synthetic yarn. This continuous processing system is a variation of the cotton processing system eliminating the processes which involved opening, cleaning, and transforming cotton fibers into laps preparatory to the carding process. This development is due to the fact that synthetic staples do not require extensive opening and cleaning as do natural fibers. The establishment has 9,792 spinning spindles, producing in excess of 175,000 Pounds of synthetic yarn weekly.

Training for production jobs in this plant is usually on-the-job. Training periods extend from weeks up to 2 years, the latter applicable to those persons engaged in setting up and repairing various machinery. No specialized training is required for entry jobs, only a general education being sufficient for communicating with coworkers and for learning the required tasks of the job. There are no definite lines of promotion; however, workers are upgraded into jobs that require more experience and skill as vacancies arise, based on their industriousness and willingness to assume responsibility. This is an equal opportunity establishment. There are no restrictions on the employment, training, and promotion of minority groups, women, or the handicapped. This establishment works three shifts.

Organization and Operations

The PLANT SUPERINTENDENT coordinates production activities for the plant. Subordinate supervisory personnel include a CARD ROOM SUPERVISOR, SPINNING ROOM SUPERVISOR, SHIPPING AND OUTSIDE FOREMAN, and MACHINIST. A SHIFT SUPERVISOR for both the second and third shifts works under the combined supervision of the CARD ROOM SUPERVISOR and SPINNING ROOM SUPERVISOR. This study was limited to the observation of production jobs.

Receiving

Synthetic fibers are shipped to the plant by manufacturers of man-made staples in boxes weighing up to 650 pounds. Fibers are unloaded from trucks and stored in the warehouse

Carding

This process as used in this establishment involves blending synthetic fibers and/or reusable waste, and feeding fibers through a distribution system into <u>carding machines</u> that produce <u>sliver</u>. Specified amounts of fibers fed into blending machines are deposited onto a conveyor from automatic weighing units attached to blending machines. Fibers are sprayed with fugitive dye tints and antistatic chemicals for identity as to type and to reduce friction in fibers during processing, and are conveyed through a piping system to automatic feeding units containing aprons with pins that feed fibers on a controlled basis to carding machines. Carding machines are equipped with several cylinders covered with metallic spikes that work in conjunction with carding drums to remove impurities from fibers, arrange fibers parallel, and produce sliver which is coiled in cans for use in the drawing process.

Drawing

This involves combining and passing several strands of sliver through two or more pairs of rollers, each of which rotate at a higher speed than the preceding pair, to attenuate the sliver.

Two phases of this process are used, namely breaker and finish drawing. In the initial step, eight slivers are fed into drawing machines that combine and straighten the fibers to produce a strand of uniform weight and size. The second phase combines eight breaker strands of sliver into one, thus improving the quality of the sliver processed. Sliver formed during the drawing process is coiled into cans for feeding into roving frames.

Roving

The purpose of this process is to combine and reduce sliver received from <u>drawing frames</u> into a continuous, slightly twisted strand called roving, and to wind roving onto bobbins for use in the spinning process. The <u>drafting rollers</u> of the <u>roving frames</u> draw out the sliver, and flyers slightly twist the roving as it is wound into bobbins.

Spinning

In this process ring <u>spinning frames</u> are used to reduce roving to yarn and to wind yarn onto bobbins. Roving from bobbins placed in the creels of spinning frames is drawn to its final size by sets of drafting rollers, twisted by <u>travelers</u> on the rings of spinning frames, and wound onto spinning bobbins.

Winding

This involves transferring yarn from spinning bobbins onto cones and spring coils through use of winding machines. A technique for joining broken ends together in specified yarn types is employed in addition to the use of hand knitters. This process, called "splicing" by management, involves gluing broken yarn ends together with a latex base compound, producing a knotless yarn.

Inspecting and Packing

Yarn packages are examined for finishing defects such as knots, soils, loose or tight winding, and absence of labels and specified color tip of cones. Ultraviolet lamps are used for detecting packages failing to meet blending specifications and for separating faultily mixed lots. Following inspection, yarn packages are wrapped in paper to prevent damage to yarn during shipment, and packed in shipping cartons. Cartons are stenciled with identifying information, weighed, strapped with steel bands, and moved to the shipping area by a conveyor.

Shipping

Customer order shipments are loaded onto trucks and transported to a central warehouse for consolidation of orders and delivery to customers of subsidiary plants, following priority of orders.

Environmental Conditions

The physical plant was constructed during the 1920's, but has been remodeled in the past 7 years. It is adequately lighted and ventilated and is clean. A cafeteria, containing a coin-operated food-and-beverage dispensing machine, is available for use by workers during breaks and lunch periods. Smoking areas are also provided and so designated to minimize fire hazards.

The noise level is considered critical as a result of the constant operation of machines throughout the plant. Automatic vacuum piping systems and overhead traveling cleaners reduce the amount of lint and other foreign matter in the carding and spinning rooms that could result in worker discomfort.

Workers handling cartons of yarn and fibers or other heavy objects work together as team members or use lifting devices and hand trucks in moving materials and supplies to prevent personal injury. Though the possibility for injuries exists for personnel working with or around machines, strict observance of safety rules and regulations rarely results in serious injury. Selected workers from each shift are trained in rendering first-aid treatment when minor injuries occur.

Special Comments

The processing of synthetic fibers into sliver using the system outlined eliminates the picking process which involves transforming fibers into laps for use in the carding process. The replacement of revolving flats with a series of rolls containing metallic spikes reduces the grinding and stripping operations usually accompanying the carding of natural fibers as synthetic fibers do not require extensive cleaning. As a result, such tasks as feeding blending machines and tending carding machines have been added to the carding process.

10

Glossary

6's to 30's: coarse to medium yarn.

Hoppers: Units containing aprons with spikes that remove compression from synthetic fibers. Several types of fibers and waste can be blended into this unit with unusable waste fibers removed by piping system.

Sliver: Loose, untwisted strand of synthetic fibers produced on carding machines and drawing frames.

Fugitive Dye: A dye which is not fast. Attenuate: To make slender or thin.

Cans: Large, cylindrical containers used to receive and hold sliver delivered from drawing frames for feeding into roving frames.

Drafting Rollers: Two or more pairs of rollers, each pair of which rotates at a higher speed than the preceding pair, serving to attenuate the roving passing between them.

Carding Machine: Machine used to remove impurities from synthetic fibers, arrange fibers parallel, and produce sliver for drawing process. The machine consists of several cylinders covered with metallic teeth that card the fibers.

Drawing Frame: Machine used to combine several strands of sliver and draw out strand to produce one of uniform weight and size.

Spinning Frame: Machine used to draw out and transform slightly twisted roving into yarn and wind yarn onto bobbins.

Roving Frame: Machine used to draw out strands of sliver and loosely twist them together to form roving.

Winding Machine: Machine used to transfer yarn from bobbins onto cones and spring coils.

Traveler: A small free-running metal ring sliding on a bar through which thread passes into other textile machine to impart a twist to the thread.